PATTERNS OF ADAPTATION AND VARIATION IN THE GREAT BASIN KANGAROO RAT

(*Dipodomys microps*)

Patterns of Adaptation and Variation in the Great Basin Kangaroo Rat
(Dipodomys microps)

by Blair A. Csuti

A contribution from the Museum of Vertebrate Zoology,
University of California, Berkeley

UNIVERSITY OF CALIFORNIA PRESS
BERKELEY • LOS ANGELES • LONDON

UNIVERSITY OF CALIFORNIA PUBLICATIONS IN ZOOLOGY

Volume 111

UNIVERSITY OF CALIFORNIA PRESS
BERKELEY AND LOS ANGELES, CALIFORNIA

UNIVERSITY OF CALIFORNIA PRESS, LTD.
LONDON, ENGLAND

ISBN 0-520-09597-9
LIBRARY OF CONGRESS CATALOG CARD NUMBER: 78-54792

©1979 BY THE REGENTS OF THE UNIVERSITY OF CALIFORNIA
PRINTED IN THE UNITED STATES OF AMERICA

Contents

List of Illustrations   vi
List of Tables   vii
Acknowledgments   viii

INTRODUCTION   1

GEOGRAPHIC VARIATION   6
    Cranial Variation, 6; Tooth Morphology, 8; Bacular Variation, 10; Kidney Anatomy, 12; Chromosomal Variation, 13; Biochemical Variation, 15; Discussion, 16

ADAPTATION FOR LIFE IN TWO HABITATS   19
    Study Sites, 19; Climate, 20; Plant Communities, 22; Faunal Communities, 23; Food Habits, 25; Feeding Experiments, 28

DISCUSSION   51
    Mechanisms of Adaptation in *Dipodomys microps*, 51; Palaeoecology of *Dipodomys microps*, 54; Biogeography of *Dipodomys microps*, 56; Implications of Geographic Variation in the Niche, 57

SUMMARY AND CONCLUSIONS   59

Appendix   61
Literature Cited   63
Plates   71

List of Illustrations

FIGURES

FIGURE 1. Range of *Dipodomys microps,* 3
FIGURE 2. Cranial measurements of *Dipodomys microps,* 7
FIGURE 3. Discriminant function analysis of cranial measurements, 9
FIGURE 4. Angle of curvature of tip of baculum, 11
FIGURE 5. Discriminant function analysis of bacular data, 12
FIGURE 6. Relative kidney weight in two populations of *Dipodomys microps,* 14
FIGURE 7. Nei distances between populations of *Dipodomys microps,* 17
FIGURE 8. Owens Valley adults, various diets, Experiment II, 33
FIGURE 9. *Coleogyne* zone adults, *Atriplex* diet, Experiment III, 37
FIGURE 10. *Coleogyne* zone adults, *Coleogyne* leaf diet, Experiment III, 37
FIGURE 11. Captive-born young, effect of early diet, Experiment III, 40
FIGURE 12. Captive-born young, effect of early diet, Experiment IV, 42
FIGURE 13. Wolf Hole adults, immediate *Atriplex*, Experiment V, 44
FIGURE 14. Wolf Hole adults, *Atriplex,* 35 days exposure, Experiment V, 44
FIGURE 15. Wolf Hole adults, *Atriplex,* 70 days exposure, Experiment V, 45
FIGURE 16. Owens Valley adults, immediate *Atriplex,* Experiment V, 45
FIGURE 17. Owens Valley adults, *Atriplex,* 70 days exposure, Experiment V, 46
FIGURE 18. Wolf Hole adults, dry seed diet, Experiment VI, 48

PLATES

PLATE 1.a. Karyotype of *Dipodomys microps microps*
       b. Karyotype of *Dipodomys microps,* Joshua Tree
PLATE 2.a. Owens Valley study area
       b. Wolf Hole study area

List of Tables

TABLE 1. Summary of cranial measurements, 8
TABLE 2. Lower incisor dimensions, 10
TABLE 3. Bacular dimensions, 11
TABLE 4. Body and kidney sizes of two samples of *Dipodomys microps,* 13
TABLE 5. Summary of karyotypes of *Dipodomys microps,* 14
TABLE 6. Genetic identity (I) and Nei distances (D), 16
TABLE 7. Summary of weather records, 21
TABLE 8. Composition of plant communities at study sites, 22
TABLE 9. Small mammal community composition, 24
TABLE 10. Results of stomach contents analysis, 27
TABLE 11. Experiment I: Wolf Hole adults, Berkeley, 31
TABLE 12. Experiment II: Wolf Hole adults, 34
TABLE 13. Experiment III: *Coleogyne* zone adults, 36
TABLE 14. Experiment III: *Atriplex* zone adults, 38
TABLE 15. Experiment III: Captive-born young, 39
TABLE 16. Experiment V: Captive-born young, 47
TABLE 17. Experiment VI: Captive-born young, dry seed diets, 49
TABLE 18. Humidity of animal rooms used in laboratory experiments, 52

Acknowledgments

I thank Dr. W. Z. Lidicker, Jr., for his support and advice during the course of this study. Dr. H. G. Baker instilled in me an appreciation for genecology during his skillful lectures on the topic. I also thank him and Dr. O. P. Pearson for their suggestions and encouragement during my stay at Berkeley. Dr. Vincent Sarich was kind enough to perform acrylamide gel electrophoresis on plasma and liver samples from my specimens. Mr. Lan A. Lester provided access to three specimens of *Dipodomys microps* from Joshua Tree National Monument deposited in the Natural History Museum of Los Angeles County. Financial support was provided by the Department of Zoology, U. C., Berkeley. Grants from the Louise Kellogg Fund and the W. F. Martens Wildlife Conservation Fund supported trips to my study areas. I thank Dr. Nello Pace for permission to use the facilities of the White Mountain Research Station.

I would like to thank Sheila M. Kortlucke for her review of the manuscript and Mark S. Hafner and Peter C. Escherich for their helpful advice. Through his friendship and cooperation, Dr. Thomas A. Ledoux made my stays at the White Mountain Research Station far more profitable than would otherwise have been the case. I thank my friends Ross Paullin and Doug Yoon for companionship in the field; my parents, Mr. and Mrs. A. S. Csuti, for their support and generosity during my many field trips; and my wife, Donna S. Csuti, for her many years of encouragement, companionship, and support.

INTRODUCTION

The complex topography of the western United States has produced a mosaic of habitat types and faunal distributions. Initially, intraspecific adaptation to these heterogeneous environments was dealt with primarily on a taxonomic level. Body size differences used to distinguish geographic races have long been assumed to be of adaptive value. Studies of physiological differences between geographically separated populations (Lindeborg, 1952; Reaka and Armitage, 1976) have emphasized the genetic basis of the observed differences. Behavioral plasticity, coupled with vagility, enable the individual animal to select from its environment those conditions favoring homeostasis, thereby minimizing phenotypic manifestations accompanying adaptation to different environments. Among plants, clues such as prostrate growth forms or sun- and shade-adapted leaf types have spurred inquiry into the underlying basis of local adaptation.

Botanists have long recognized the interplay between genetic response and phenotypic plasticity in the formation of ecological races (=ecotypes). Plants possess inherent advantages over animals as candidates for studies concerning mechanisms of adaptation. Not only are reciprocal transplants practical, but clones of genetically identical individuals can often be propagated, standardizing one of the important variables under consideration. It was, therefore, no accident that the term genecology (Greek, *genos* = race + ecology) was coined by the Swedish botanist Göte Turesson (1923) to describe the study of local adaptation following his early work (1919) on the growth habits of maritime plants. From its inception, it has been the aim of genecology to investigate geographic patterns of local adaptation and to determine their hereditary and environmental components. Although environmentally inducible variation has come to be regarded as a secondary mechanism of adaptation by plant genecologists (Heslop-Harrison, 1964), Turesson (1919) began his investigations with the observation that direct environmental action could induce in some varieties of *Atriplex* species adaptations indistinguishable from those resulting from genetic differentiation in other varieties.

The recognition that variation had two possible bases, and the subsequent experiments seeking to clarify the contributions of each component, launched the new discipline of genecology. Gregor (1944, 1946) attempted to further refine the categories of observed variation, and described clinal variation of adaptive characters. Exhaustive studies of the mechanisms underlying adaptation and variation in plant morphology and phenology were undertaken by Clausen and his associates (Clausen, Keck, and Hiesey, 1940, 1948; Clausen and Hiesey, 1958) and were later extended to include physiological traits in plants (Mooney and Shropshire, 1967; Al-Ani et al., 1972). Although Clausen et al. (1940, 1948) concluded that variation is primarily accomplished by genetic mechanisms, further work (Mooney and Shropshire, 1967) has found both phenotypic (in *Encelia californica*) and genotypic (in *Polygonum bistortoides*) mechanisms responsible for adaptation to differing environments.

Due to their cultivability, plants were natural candidates for pioneering research in genecology. Perhaps because of the difficulty involved in maintaining sample populations, there have been few attempts to analyze the relative contributions of genetic background and environmental response to spatial variation in adaptive strategy among populations of animal species. Sumner (1924, 1932) carried on extensive breeding experiments with *Peromyscus* in an attempt to determine the basis of morphological variation. He found rearing in different thermal environments produced only minor effects on coat color and external measurements. Similarly, Sumner's assistant, Ross (1930), found no intraspecific difference in water consumption in *Peromyscus maniculatus* from different habitats. Lindeborg (1952) succeeded in demonstrating variation in resistance to water stress among ecological races of *Peromyscus,* although he assumed this to be genetically controlled. Harrison (1959) summarized work on mammals, indicating that changes in adult size resulting from different rearing temperatures may be of adaptive significance. Recently, there has been some suggestion (Mason, 1974; Lynch *et al.,* 1976) that adaptive variation within species may stem from both ecotypic and ecophenic factors.

Hutchinson (1957) distinguished between the fundamental and the realized niche of a species. Implicit in this formalization of the niche concept is the requirement that spatial changes in community parameters (competitors, climatic factors, resources, etc.) will result in geographic variation in the realized niche. Frequently, predictive theories of desert rodent community structure and function have been developed with little regard for the potential of spatial modification of the niche by component species (Rosenzweig and Winakur, 1969; Rosenzweig *et al.,* 1975; Brown, 1975). By applying the principles of genecological investigation to a study of intraspecific patterns of local adaptation in a desert rodent, I hope to demonstrate not only that geographic niche variation occurs in animal species through both hereditary and non-hereditary mechanisms, but that such variation enables a species to exploit a broad spectrum of habitats by displaying plasticity in resource requirements and concomitant community interactions.

Rodents of the family Heteromyidae form a major component of the small mammal fauna of the open, arid scrublands of western North America. It is not unusual to find six or more species of the genera *Perognathus, Microdipodops,* and *Dipodomys* in apparent sympatry (Hall, 1946). Reichman (1975) and Nelson and Chew (1977) document the presence of an abundant seed reservoir in desert biomes. This family of nocturnal rodents displays specializations for exploiting this resource base. The development of saltatorial and ricochetal locomotion, coupled with external cheek pouches, allows efficient foraging over large areas while minimizing time spent exposed to predation. The coexistence of so many potentially competing species has recently invited detailed studies of these communities (Rosenzweig and Winakur, 1969; Brown, 1973, 1975).

There are 21 currently recognized species in the genus *Dipodomys,* which shows extreme development of the saltatorial mode of locomotion within the family. Members of the genus range throughout the western half of the continent from southern Canada to Mexico, but are most diverse in the southwestern United States. The relationships among species of the genus have been the subject of long debate (Grinnell, 1922; Setzer, 1949; Lidicker, 1960a). The present study involves the development of a pattern of habitat-specific adaptations in *Dipodomys microps;* although the affinities of *D. microps* remained clouded for much of its history, recent studies (Johnson and Selander, 1971; Best and Schnell, 1974; Stock, 1974) have convincingly placed it with the *heermanni* group kangaroo rats. Over half the genus is included in this group, most of whose species are found in the coastal mountains and Mojave Desert of southern California. *Dipodomys microps* ranges eastward from this region throughout the Great Basin (fig. 1).

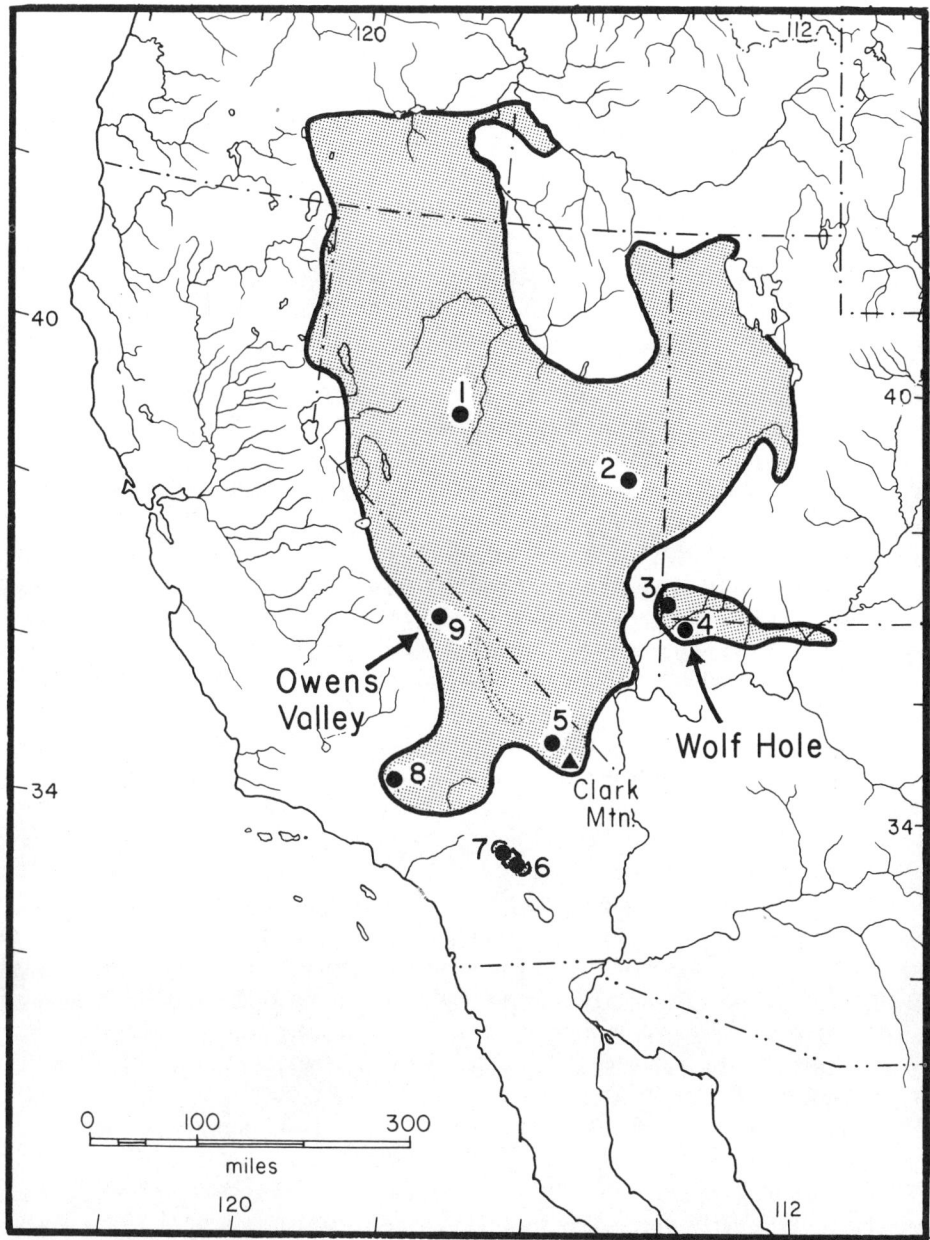

FIG. 1. Range of *Dipodomys microps* showing location of primary study areas. Specimens were collected at the following localities (in clockwise order, northernmost locality first): 1–2 mi. W Railroad Pass, Smith Creek Valley, Lander Co., Nevada; 2–5½ mi. NW Shoshone, White Pine Co., Nevada; 3–W slope Beaverdam Mountains, 3800 ft., Washington Co., Utah; 4–10 mi. N Wolf Hole, Mohave Co., Arizona; 5–½ mi. W Horse Thief Springs, Kingston Range, San Bernardino Co., California; 6–1¼ mi. NE Stubby Springs, 4750 ft., Joshua Tree National Monument, Riverside Co., California; 7–3 mi. NW Yucca Valley, San Bernardino Co., California; 8–6 mi. N Lancaster, Los Angeles Co., California; 9–2 mi. E Big Pine, Inyo Co., California.

Within the *heermanni* group there exist morphological, karyotypic, and ecological grounds for recognition of two subdivisions, first suggested by Lidicker (1960a):

HEERMANNI GROUP

heermanni subgroup	*agilis* subgroup
heermanni	agilis
ingens	microps
panamintinus	venustus
stephensi	elephantinus
gravipes	paralius
	peninsularis

Species of the *heermanni* subgroup have broad maxillary arches (=broad-faced), a large percentage of their autosomes are acrocentric, and they are most often found in open scrub or grassland. Representatives of the *agilis* subgroup have narrowly spreading maxillary arches (=narrow-faced), a primarily biarmed karyotype, and are typical of closed habitats, such as chaparral-covered slopes. Johnson and Selander (1971) suggest *D. microps* may be intermediate between the *heermanni* and *agilis* subgroups, while Best and Schnell (1974) and Stock (1974) assign the species to the *agilis* subgroup. Considering the available evidence, it appears safe to assume that *D. microps* originated from a *heermanni* group ancestor in the semi-desert regions of California. Since *D. microps* is narrow-faced, and since bacular and karyologic evidence relate it to the *agilis* subgroup, I consider it an early offshoot of that subgroup.

Kangaroo rats are notable in that some species have the ability to survive indefinitely on a dry seed diet without access to any source of moisture (Schmidt-Nielsen, K., 1964). Food habit studies (Vorhies and Taylor, 1922; Tappe, 1941; Flake, 1973; Alcoze and Zimmerman, 1973) reveal that kangaroo rats are primarily granivorous, with some seasonal tendency to take insects and green vegetation. Kenagy (1973a, b) has addressed the problem of niche separation among coexisting kangaroo rats of the desert rodent community in the Owens Valley, Inyo Co., California. Surprisingly, his report indicated that *D. microps* may escape competition for seed resources with *D. merriami* by becoming phytophagous; it has evolved specialized adaptations for feeding on the leaves of saltbush (*Atriplex confertifolia*, Chenopodiaceae). The concentration of electrolytes in the epithelium of *Atriplex* (unless otherwise specified, *Atriplex* will refer to *A. confertifolia*) leaves renders them unpalatable to most browsing species. Livestock will browse on *Atriplex*, but only if adequate drinking water is available to dissipate the salt-load acquired while feeding (Wilson, 1966a, b). In contrast, *D. microps* uses the sharp cutting edges of its unique chisel-shaped lower incisors (fig. 2) to remove the hypersaline epithelium, feeding only on the more nutritious interior of the leaf (Kenagy, 1972, 1973b).

The population of *D. microps* studied by Kenagy (1972, 1973a, b) in the Owens Valley (fig. 1) occurs in a habitat often described as typical for the species (Grinnell, 1933): alkali flats surrounding the dry basin of a Pleistocene lake. The flora (Shadscale Scrub Community of Munz and Keck, 1959) is dominated by low shrubs of the goosefoot family (Chenopodiaceae), primarily *A. confertifolia*. The disjunct southeastern populations of *D. microps*, on the other hand, can also be found on the slopes of desert mountain ranges within the blackbush (*Coleogyne ramosissima*, Rosaceae) zone, such as at my Wolf Hole study site (fig. 1) in northwestern Arizona, at Joshua Tree National Monument, and in the eastern San Bernardino Mountains. Billings (1949) points out a blackbush belt, often mixed with yucca or juniper, but rarely with sagebrush, at 3500 to 5000 ft lying between Creosote Bush Scrub or Shadscale Scrub and Sagebrush Scrub (Munz and Keck; 1959) on the mountain slopes of the southern Great Basin. *Atriplex confertifolia* is absent from this belt, being found at lower elevations, and at many localities *D. microps* is abundant despite the absence of this source of food.

Since *D. microps* has been characterized as a leaf-eater over part of its range, and since shrubs in the *Coleogyne* zone are sometimes completely deciduous (Beatley, 1976b), it is apparent that the food niche of this species varies spatially. Since *Atriplex* foraging involves concomitant physiological and behavioral adaptations (Kenagy, 1973b), use of this food item may serve as an indicator of differences in realized niche among populations of *D. microps*. Food competition has been held an important factor in desert rodent community structure (Rosenzweig *et al.*, 1975). If *D. microps* exhibits significant geographic variation in food niche, it can be inferred that its role in community dynamics differs spatially and that no single illustration of heteromyid rodent community structure involving this species can have more than regional applicability.

Hall and Dale (1939) have presented the only taxonomic revision of *Dipodomys microps*. In the following section I will review several quantitative indicators of geographic variation in *D. microps* to evaluate the available indices of genetic similarity among the populations I sampled. To distinguish genetic from environmental components of variation in food niche, both adults and lab-reared young from populations exhibiting differences in resource use were tested in a variety of laboratory experiments, which are presented in the second section. In the concluding discussion I will consider the relative contributions of genetic and nongenetic factors to the niche dynamics of *Dipodomys microps*. Finally, I will propose a sequence of events which may have led to the evolution of ecological polymorphism in this species.

GEOGRAPHIC VARIATION

Dipodomys microps was first described by Merriam (1904). Hall and Dale (1939) revised the species, recognizing 11 subspecies, distinguishable on skin and skull characters. Hall and Kelson (1959) recognized 14 subspecies, although this number was tentatively reduced to 13 by Stock (1970). Taxonomists have long recognized that the description of geographic races (or subspecies) implies divergence in genetic composition. However, the relative amount of intraspecific variation among populations and its relationship to ecological parameters has received little attention. Recently, variation in several additional morphological and biochemical characters has been investigated in *Dipodomys* to clarify taxonomic relationships (Johnson and Selander, 1971; Best and Schnell, 1974; Stock, 1974). While these studies deal with the entire genus, they contain information on some populations of *D. microps*. In the following sections I will review the current assessment of geographic variation in *D. microps*, incorporating my own data where appropriate. Since each type of variation considered—biochemical, morphological, or karyotypic—attempts to sample the genetic relatedness of populations from different habitats, the use of these indicators may make it possible to estimate how much of the geographic variation in realized niche within the species is the result of genetic differentiation and how much is due to physiological or developmental flexibility. Specimens examined are listed in the appendix.

CRANIAL VARIATION

The morphometric study by Hall and Dale (1939) was based on 1149 specimens. No specimens of *D. microps* were known from the mountain slopes of southern California at that time. As these populations were discovered, they were assigned to the subspecies *occidentalis* on the basis of location (Johnson et al., 1948; Miller and Stebbins, 1964). I sampled representative populations from this region. Eight cranial measurements representing all diagnostic skull dimensions used by Grinnell (1922) and Hall and Dale (1939) were taken with the aid of dial calipers. Following Lidicker (1960a:128), only measurements from adult specimens were used. Adults have complete permanent dentition, with all teeth showing some wear, and the auditory bullae are at least partly translucent. The measurements used are illustrated in figure 2. Hall and Dale (1939) found no significant secondary sexual variation in *D. microps*. I therefore followed the method of Genoways and Jones (1971), combining data from both sexes, but keeping the proportion of males and females similar in each sample. All specimens examined were from the collection of the Museum of Vertebrate Zoology, University of California, Berkeley, unless otherwise stated.

The Berkeley FSU-CAL version of the BMD07M program for stepwise discriminant function analysis was employed in analysis of these data. The eleven specimens from Joshua Tree

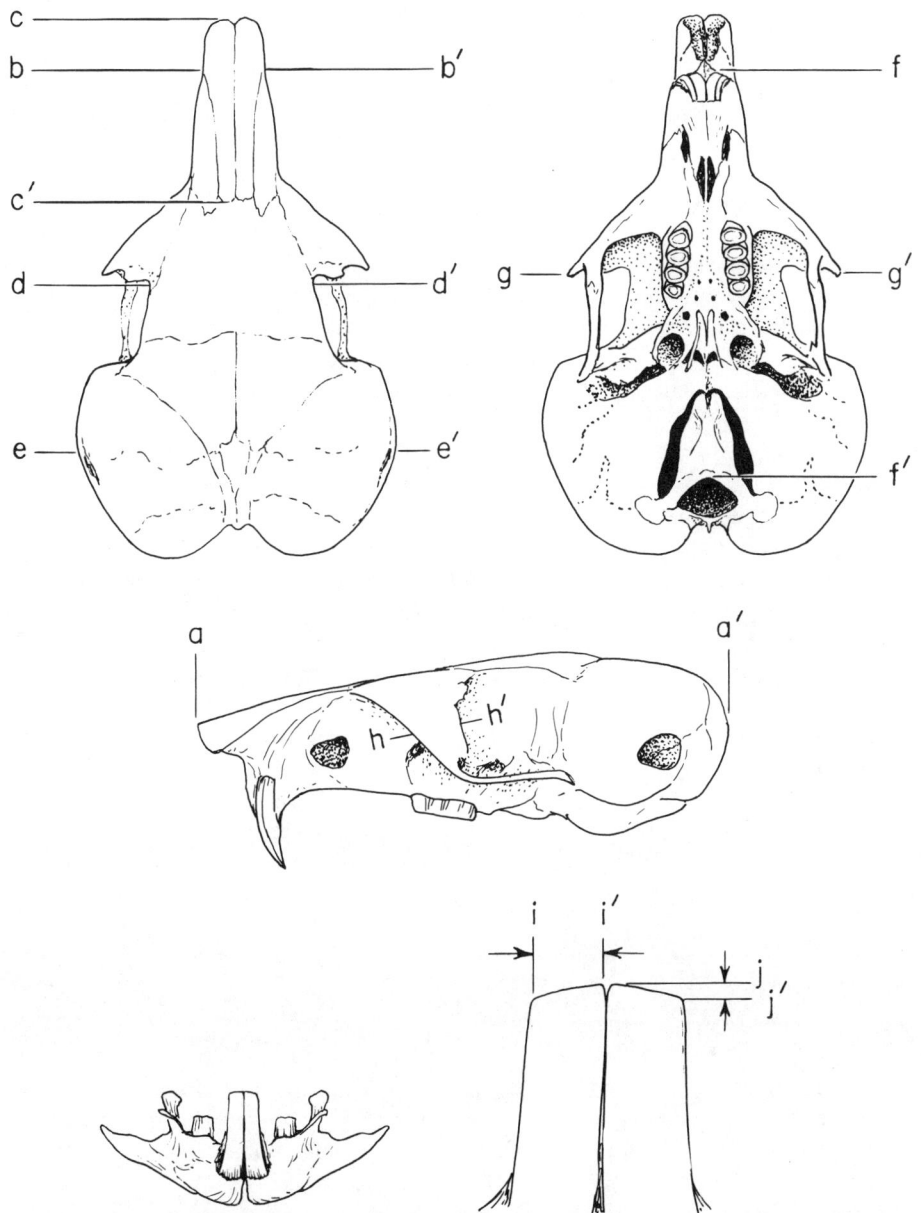

FIG. 2. Cranial measurements of *Dipodomys microps*. Dorsal, ventral, and lateral views of skull (MVZ 56124) showing cranial measurements used in this study. a, a', greatest length of skull; b, b', rostral width; c, c', nasal length; d, d', interorbital width; e, e', breadth of skull across bullae; f, f', basal length; g, g', maxillary breadth; h, h', width of maxillary arch; i, i', width of right lower incisor; j, j', distance from distal edge of lower incisor to outer distal corner.

National Monument and the two from Clark Mountain were designated as unknowns and assigned to reference groups consisting of specimens of *D. m. microps* (n=12), *D. m. celsus* (n=12), and *D. m. occidentalis* (n=18). Table 1 summarizes mensural data for the specimens examined. The measurements of individual specimens and their probability of inclusion in reference groups are presented elsewhere (Csuti, 1977). Cluster analysis along the first two canonical variables is illustrated in figure 3. These data indicate strong divergence between the western populations of *D. m. microps* and the eastern populations of *D. m. celsus*. Specimens of *D. m. occidentalis* occupy an intermediate position. All specimens from Joshua Tree National Monument (=Joshua Tree) cluster in an intermediate position and are assigned to the *occidentalis* group with probabilities ranging from 0.61 to 0.99. This assessment agrees with that of Miller and Stebbins (1964). On the basis of this analysis, the two specimens from Clark Mountain fall within the range of *D. m. celsus*, suggesting the taxonomic status of this isolated population should be reexamined.

TOOTH MORPHOLOGY

Landry (1970) presents evidence that the tooth and jaw mechanisms of rodents are efficient devices for handling a wide variety of food items and may have been in large part responsible for the adaptive radiation of the Rodentia. Examples are presented in which rodents with varied diets display little or no modification of the basic feeding apparatus. Al-

TABLE 1. SUMMARY OF CRANIAL MEASUREMENTS OF *DIPODOMYS MICROPS*
(in millimeters)

Sample	Greatest length of skull	Rostral width	Nasal length	Interorbital breadth	Breadth of skull across bullae	Basal length	Maxillary breadth	Width of maxillary arch
D. m. microps (n=12)								
mean	35.59	3.25	12.50	11.53	22.40	25.57	18.59	3.20
± SD	.69	.21	.51	.51	.67	.49	.62	.30
D. m. occidentalis (n=18)								
mean	36.82	3.47	12.80	11.79	23.74	26.46	19.49	3.24
± SD	.87	.19	.43	.48	.60	.51	.69	.28
D. m. celsus (n=12)								
mean	38.75	3.76	13.72	12.26	24.48	27.60	20.14	3.59
± SD	.86	.22	.70	.22	.47	.76	.77	.28
Joshua Tree (n=11)								
mean	36.72	3.48	12.38	12.20	24.13	26.24	19.55	3.26
± SD	.61	.19	.47	.35	.50	.67	.63	.30
Clark Mtn. (n=2)								
mean	39.37	3.91	13.82	12.19	24.69	28.09	20.65	4.14

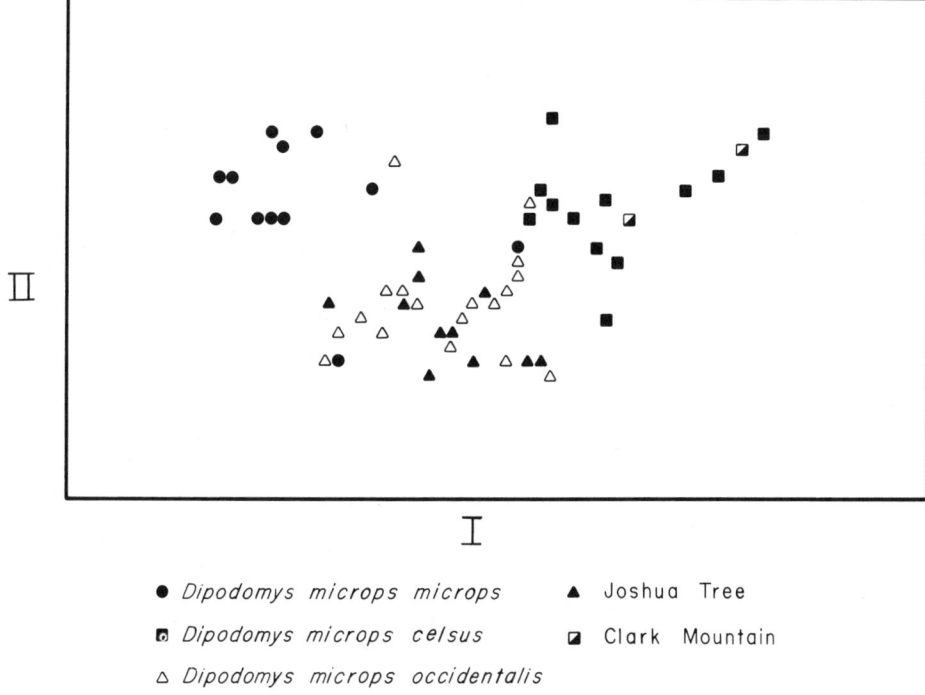

FIG. 3. Discriminant function analysis of eight cranial measurements of *Dipodomys microps* samples. Horizontal axis = first canonical axis, vertical axis = second canonical axis.

though the basic jaw musculature and tooth morphology of *D. microps* seems not to differ from that of its congeners, Hall and Dale (1939) point out the uniqueness of the lower incisors. All other *Dipodomys* share an awl-shaped lower incisor, with a convex anterior surface and a roughly parabolic distal edge. *Dipodomys microps* is distinctive in its possession of chisel-shaped lower incisors with flat anterior faces and distal edges that are nearly flat—i.e., perpendicular to the long axis of the tooth. Kenagy (1973b) presented evidence that the lower incisors play an essential role in the leaf-shaving behavior pattern which allows the species to use *Atriplex* leaves as a year-round food source in the Owens Valley. The possibility exists that reduced selection pressure for the chisel-shaped lower incisor may result in increased variation of tooth morphology in those parts of the range where *Atriplex* leaves are absent from the diet. To investigate this possibility, I examined the morphology of the lower incisors in populations from both *Atriplex* and *Coleogyne* habitats.

A twenty-power optical comparator was used to project a silhouette of the lower incisor onto a frosted glass screen. The width of the right lower incisor and the distance from its distal edge to the outer distal corner were measured with the aid of a graduated stage (fig. 2). It was not possible to standardize any measurement of the curvature of the anterior face of the incisor using this device.

Results are presented in table 2. No significant difference between means was found between the populations examined, nor was any increased variation detected in blackbush samples (coefficient of variation = standard deviation x 100/mean, Sokal and Rohlf, 1969).

TABLE 2. LOWER INCISOR DIMENSIONS
(in millimeters)

	Atriplex area D. m. centralis n = 21	Blackbush area D. m. celsus n = 21
Width of Tooth		
x̄	0.95	0.93
SD	±0.10	±0.08
SE	0.02	0.02
CV	10.6%	8.9%
Curvature of distal edge		
x̄	0.26	0.26
SD	±0.10	±0.10
SE	0.02	0.02
CV	37.7%	38.5%

BACULAR VARIATION

The dimensions and shape of the baculum have been used as a taxonomic indicator in the genus *Dipodomys* (Lidicker, 1960b; Kelly, 1969; Best and Schnell, 1974). Intraspecific geographic variation in bacular dimensions is generally considered negligible. Although few samples of *D. microps* bacula were available, the work of Best and Schnell (1974) indicates an analysis based on relatively small sample sizes may be justified if results are viewed conservatively. Therefore, I measured the available adult specimens from southern populations of *D. microps* to search for possible significant interpopulation differences in size or shape of the baculum.

The fresh or dried phallus of each specimen was prepared according to the method described by Lidicker (1960b). Bacular measurements were read from a digital display connected to the micrometer stage of a Nikon dissecting microscope. In addition to the standard bacular measurements of length, width, and height used by Best and Schnell (1974), the angle of curvature of the tip of the baculum, as illustrated in figure 4, was measured with the aid of an optical goniometer on a Wild M5 dissecting microscope. A summary of bacular measurements is presented in table 3. Measurements of individual specimens and their probability of inclusion in reference groups are presented in Csuti (1977).

These data were analyzed by means of the Berkeley FSU-CAL version of the BMD07M program for stepwise discriminant function analysis. Only slight discrimination is possible among the populations sampled if the angular measurement is excluded from the analysis. However, an analysis including this character (fig. 5) shows considerable separation between *D. m. microps* and *D. m. celsus* samples, with angles of curvature of 68.5° and 76.5° respectively. Mean angle of curvature for the two specimens from Clark Mountain is 70°; that of the Joshua Tree specimens is 73°; and that of the Yucca Valley individual, a new locality for the species, is 77.7°. These results indicate this character may be of considerable systematic value.

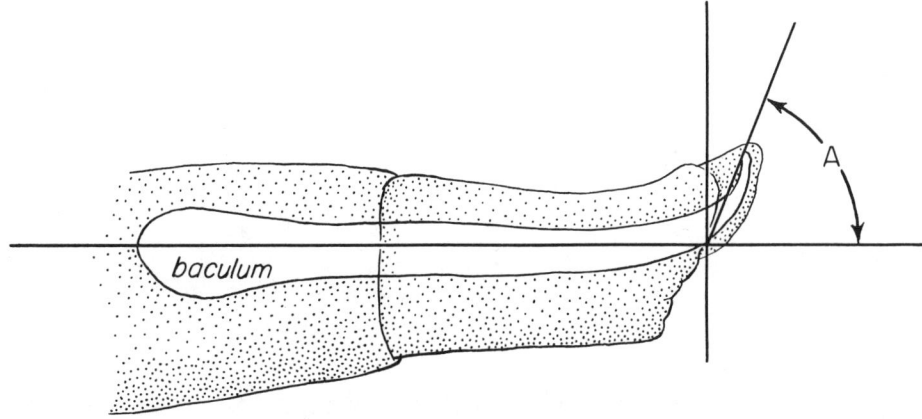

FIG. 4. Angle of curvature of tip of baculum. Lateral view of the phallus and baculum of *Dipodomys microps* (MVZ 148434) illustrating the angle used to quantify the curvature of the tip of the baculum. The crosshairs of an optical goniometer were placed so the long axis of the crosshair (measuring pointer) bisected the baculum and the perpendicular crosshair intersected the long crosshair at the point it exited the anterior edge of the baculum, as detected through the transparent glans. The perpendicular crosshair was then rotated until it passed through the tip of the baculum and angle A was read directly from the goniometer scale.

TABLE 3. BACULAR DIMENSIONS OF *DIPODOMYS MICROPS*
(Angular measurements given in degrees, linear measurements in millimeters)

Sample	n	Angle of curvature	Length of shaft	Height of base	Width of base
Dipodomys microps microps					
mean	7	68.4	10.39	1.56	1.36
± SD		3.4	.42	.19	.14
D. m. occidentalis (Clark Mtn.)					
mean	2	70.2	10.79	1.53	1.30
± SD		1.8	.16	.14	.13
D. m. celsus (Wolf Hole)					
mean	5	76.5	10.61	1.65	1.49.
± SD		3.3	.31	.14	.13
Joshua Tree					
mean	3	73.0	10.40	1.42	1.39
± SD		1.5	.32	.13	.08
Yucca Valley	1	77.7	10.43	1.38	1.47

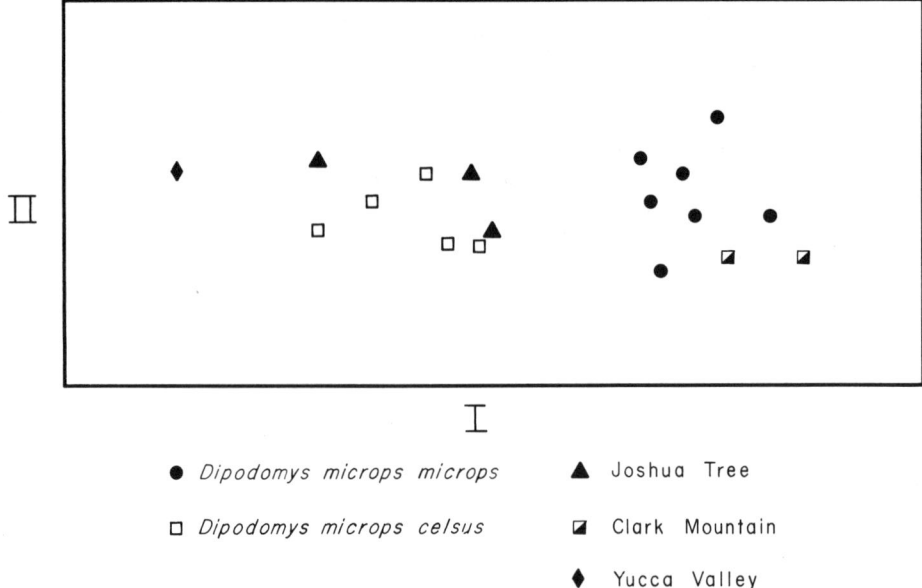

FIG. 5. Discriminant function analysis of four bacular measurements of *Dipodomys microps* samples. Horizontal axis = first canonical axis, vertical axis = second canonical axis.

The three specimens from Joshua Tree and the one from Yucca Valley were assigned to the race *celsus* with a probability of 100%. This similarity between the Wolf Hole and the San Bernardino Mountain populations may reflect conservatism in the angle of curvature, a high degree of relatedness, or convergence in this character. However, the difference detected between Owens Valley (*D. m. microps*) and Wolf Hole (*D. m. celsus*) populations provides further evidence that these peripheral populations are genetically divergent.

KIDNEY ANATOMY

Species of the genus *Dipodomys* vary widely in their ability to maintain body weight on a regime that does not include free water or succulent vegetation. While the Schmidt-Nielsens (1952) have documented the ability of *D. merriami* to survive indefinitely without water, Carpenter (1966) has demonstrated the need of *D. agilis* for some moisture in the diet, as has Church (1969) for *D. venustus*. Kenagy (1973b) studied *D. microps* in the Owens Valley and reported that it was poorly adapted to periods of water deprivation. Since populations of *D. microps* on the southern edge of the range must survive parts of the year without access to green vegetation, whereas the Owens Valley population consumes quantities of succulent but salt-laden leaves throughout the year, one may predict an intraspecific difference in water conservation abilities between them.

Although there are many behavioral and physiological adaptations involved in water conservation, the concentrating ability of the kidney is one of the most important. Carpenter (1969), Greegor (1975), and Fleming (1977) correlated aspects of kidney morphology with concentrating ability. In the present study, kidney weight relative to body weight was used as an estimate of renal capabilities. Kidney weights were recorded for samples of *D. microps* populations from two different habitats. Kidneys removed from freshly killed or frozen adult specimens were weighed to the nearest milligram on a torsion balance. A Student's t-test of male versus female specimens revealed no significant differences, therefore data for the sexes were combined. In all cases the right kidney was used for analysis.

Table 4 summarizes the mensural data gathered on kidney samples. The weight of the kidney is plotted against body weight in figure 6. The kidney weight of Owens Valley specimens is greater than that of Wolf Hole specimens, whereas their body weight is significantly smaller. There is no overlap in relative kidney weight. This striking anatomical difference provides further evidence that these populations have adapted to their different resource bases. Brownfield and Wunder (1976) suggest that relative medullary area may represent the best morphological index of renal capabilities. Further work with *D. microps* kidneys is planned to investigate the possible correlation of morphological and histological features of the kidney with maximal urine-concentrating ability.

TABLE 4. BODY AND KIDNEY SIZES OF TWO SAMPLES OF *DIPODOMYS MICROPS*

	D. m. microps (Owens Valley)	*D. m. celsus* (Wolf Hole)
	n = 10	n = 13
Body Weight (g)	53.5±4.4	69.8±9.8
Kidney Weight (mg)	473±58	349±40
Relative Kidney Weight (mg kidney/g body)	8.82±.59	5.08±.81

Figures represent means ± standard deviation.
Relative kidney weights differ between localities at $p > .01$ using Student's t-test.

CHROMOSOMAL VARIATION

Chromosomal morphology has become available in recent years as an indicator of taxonomic relationships (Patton, 1967, 1969). Stock (1974) surveyed karyotypic variation in the genus *Dipodomys* and proposed a phylogeny based on chromosomal evidence. Aside from the two localities examined by Stock (1974) in Washington Co., Utah, and Lincoln Co., Nevada, the only other published record of a *Dipodomys microps* karyotype is that of Csuti (1971). These published records indicate an absence of intraspecific karyotypic variation in the species. Nevertheless, intraspecific variation in karyotype has been frequently found in mammalian species. I therefore undertook a more thorough survey of *D. microps* populations to investigate potential variation in this character.

Chromosome slides were prepared by a modification of the technique described by Patton (1967), and are deposited in the collection of the Museum of Vertebrate Zoology. Standard museum study skins and skulls were prepared from all specimens examined and are also deposited in that institution. Karyotypes were prepared from photomicrographs of well-spread cells taken at 1200x magnification.

Chromosomal morphology of *D. microps* populations I sampled is summarized in table 5. A major karyotypic difference was detected in the population from Joshua Tree National Monument (plate 1b). All other populations agree with the previously described karyotype (plate 1a). The specimen taken near Yucca Valley, representing an isolated population in the blackbush zone of the eastern San Bernardino Mountains 32 km northwest of the karyotypically distinct Joshua Tree National Monument population, shares the common karyotype with northern and eastern populations.

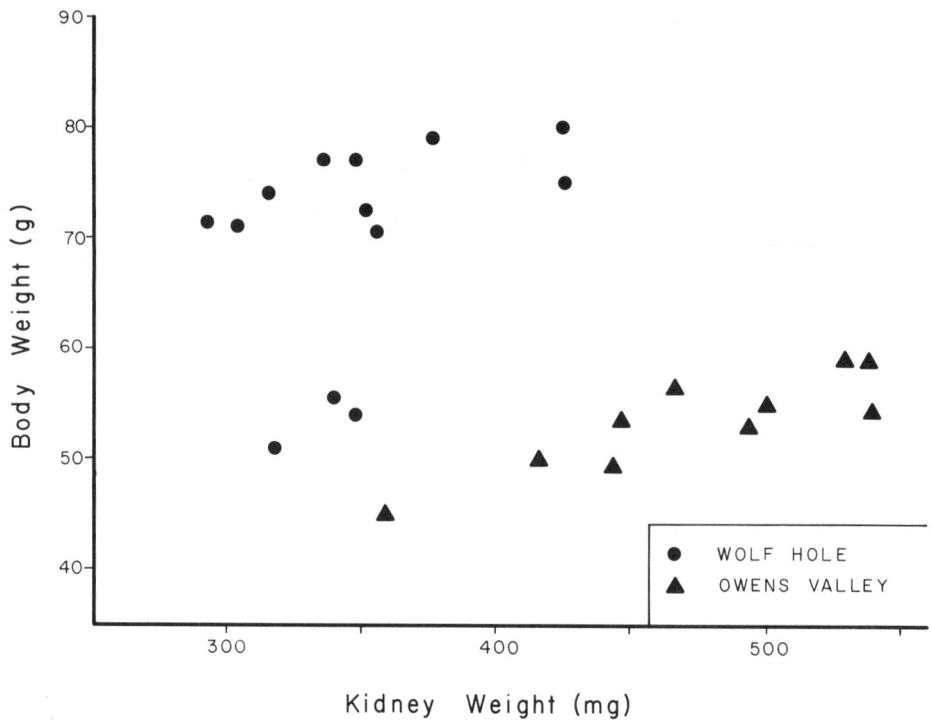

FIG. 6. Relative kidney weight in two populations of *Dipodomys microps*.

TABLE 5. SUMMARY OF KARYOTYPES OF *DIPODOMYS MICROPS**

Population	♂	♀	2n	\multicolumn{4}{c	}{Autosomes}	X	Y	FN
				M	SM	ST	A			
Dipodomys microps microps	7	3	60	13	16			M	A	116
Dipodomys microps occidentalis	--	2	60	13	16			--	--	116
Dipodomys microps centralis	--	1	60	13	16			--	--	116
Dipodomys microps celsus	2	1	60	13	16			M	A	116
Dipodomys microps woodburyi	1	1	60	13	16			M	A	116
Dipodomys microps (Yucca Valley)	--	1	60	13	16			--	--	116
Dipodomys microps (Joshua Tree)	3	3	60	8	5	3	13	M	A	90

*M = metacentric, SM = submetacentric, ST = subtelocentric, A = acrocentric, FN = fundamental number.

The common *D. microps* karyotype has been described earlier (Csuti, 1971; Stock, 1974). My recent preparations of this karyotype indicate the smallest element in the series of biarmed autosomes typically has much reduced second arms, appearing acrocentric (or telocentric) in many cases. Because of the small size of this chromosome, the influence of the degree of contraction on interpretation, and the presence of visible second arms in some preparations, this chromosome was scored as biarmed. The karyotype of the population from Joshua Tree National Monument is characterized as follows: diploid number = 60, number of autosomal arms (Fundamental Number of Matthey, 1951) = 90. There are eight metacentric pairs, five submetacentric pairs, three subtelocentric pairs, and 13 acrocentric pairs of autosomes. The X chromosomes are the largest pair of submetacentric chromosomes and the third largest of all biarmed pairs. The Y chromosome is acrocentric.

Based only on the karyotypic evidence presented here, it is not possible to determine the course of chromosome evolution in *D. microps;* however, since both karyotypes have a diploid number of 60, it seems likely that inversions may be involved. The Joshua Tree form may represent a relict of an ancestral type which has persisted on a mountain island surrounded by a sea of Lower Sonoran desert, or it may be a recently derived karyotype in a population which invaded the San Bernardino Mountains from the north or east. In either case, chromosomal changes do not seem to be environmentally related in this species.

BIOCHEMICAL VARIATION

Since the 1930's, systematists have recognized that by quantifying similarities in external morphology, they were attempting to assess the genetic distance between populations. In the last decade, techniques have been developed to compare primary gene products (i.e., proteins) in an effort to measure similarity between populations at the biochemical level (Selander *et al.,* 1971). Using this technique, Johnson and Selander (1971) investigated the genus *Dipodomys.* Seven populations of *D. microps* were sampled and a mean coefficient of intraspecific genetic similarity of 0.994 was calculated. Samples from the extreme southern portion of the range were not included in their analysis of the species. Recently Sarich (1977) has presented evidence that systematic information of comparable quality can be obtained using small sample sizes from each population surveyed. His system uses acrylamide gel electrophoresis to compare all plasma proteins or liver esterases of representative specimens on a single gel. Although Sarich (1977) recognizes the need for caution in assigning an absolute time scale to the genetic distances calculated, relative genetic distance between a group of populations can be quickly and easily scored.

Plasma and liver samples were extracted from representatives of nine populations from the southern half of the range of *D. microps.* Both plasma protein and liver esterase gels were scored for each set of specimens being compared. The following criteria were used when scoring gels: (1) each specimen was compared pairwise only with adjacent and next-to-adjacent specimens; (2) patterns of multiple bands always present as a unit throughout the taxon were scored as a unit difference, rather than individually; (3) plasma bands were scored only if a comparable band appeared in each of the two samples being compared; (4) liver esterase bands were scored on the basis of total bands present, the absence of a band being scored as a dissimilarity; (5) moderate intensity differences were presumed to result from concentration effects and were neglected in scoring; (6) a locus polymorphic for two or more alleles was scored as a dissimilarity only if the migration rate for any allele in the system varied, not if the presence of one or another allele of a polymorphic locus common to all populations in the taxon varied between individuals. Genetic relatedness, *I,* was estimated by taking the percentage of shared alleles compared to the total number of alleles scored. A Nei Distance (Nei, 1971), *D,* was calculated between samples using the formula, $D = -\ln I$. Samples from all specimens are deposited in the Frozen Tissue Collection of the Museum of Vertebrate Zoology, University of California, Berkeley.

Results of the analysis of plasma protein and liver esterase electrophoresis are presented in table 6. Since individuals could not be scored against other specimens separated by more than one column on the gels, this matrix is incomplete. The degree of intrapopulation similarity was assessed in specimens from two localities. These data indicate relatedness (*I*) within the same population is 0.86. Average relatedness between all *D. microps* populations was scored

TABLE 6. GENETIC IDENTITY (*I*) AND NEI DISTANCES (*D*) BETWEEN *DIPODOMYS MICROPS* POPULATIONS AS INDICATED BY ACRYLAMIDE GEL ELECTROPHORESIS*

Sample	Joshua Tree	Yucca Valley	Lancaster	Big Pine	Kingston Range	Beaverdam Mts.	Wolf Hole	Smith Creek Valley	Shoshone
Joshua Tree — *D. m. ssp.*		.19	.33	.25	--	.56	.55	.45	.40
Yucca Valley — *D. m. ssp.*	.83		--	.34	--	--	--	--	--
Lancaster — *D. m. microps*	.73	--		.30	.49	--	.46	--	--
Big Pine — *D. m. microps*	.78	.71	.74		.48	.26	.45	.34	--
Kingston Range — *D. m. occidentalis*	--	--	.61	.62		.45	.58	--	--
Beaverdam Mts. — *D. m. woodburyi*	.57	--	--	.77	.64		.34	.48	.37
Wolf Hole — *D. m. celsus*	.58	--	.63	.64	.56	.71		--	.25
Smith Creek Valley — *D. m. occidentalis*	.64	--	--	.71	--	.61	--		.17
Shoshone — *D. m. centralis*	.67	--	--	--	--	.69	.78	.84	

D (upper triangle) / *I* (lower triangle)

*An average of 27 (range 21-38) alleles were scored for each comparison. This variation resulted from differences in specimen quality and the number of visible plasma bands. See text for explanation of scoring criteria.

as 0.68 (range 0.56-0.83). Figure 7 illustrates the calculated genetic distances, *D*, between the populations of *D. microps* I sampled.

The degree of relatedness between populations of *D. microps* is high and is generally correlated with geographic distance between populations. The distance between nearby populations is 0.37 or less. Physical barriers to gene flow are not illustrated on figure 7. The relatively large genetic distance between neighboring and otherwise similar populations of *D. microps* from the Beaverdam Wash (Locality 3) and Wolf Hole (Locality 4) may be the result of their separation by the Beaverdam and Virgin Mountains.

The Yucca Valley and Joshua Tree populations, 32 km apart, share 83% of their alleles. The similarity among the three individuals scored from the Joshua Tree population alone ranges from 82 to 91%. Within this system of analysis, the Yucca Valley individual could easily represent the same gene pool as the Joshua Tree individuals. These recently discovered blackbush zone populations display a higher degree of similarity to the neighboring *D. m. microps* populations than they do to *D. m. celsus*. Their enzymatic affinities lie with the western *Atriplex* zone populations of the species rather than with those *Coleogyne* zone populations found on the mountain slopes of Arizona and Utah.

The data gathered here agree with Johnson and Selander's (1971) conclusion that the species displays little geographic variation. The greater degree of intraspecific variation detected by acrylamide gel electrophoresis suggests that this technique is more appropriate for sampling intraspecific variation in *Dipodomys* species.

DISCUSSION

In the preceding sections the degree of genetic relatedness within the southern populations of *D. microps* was assessed through evidence from six different indicators, including

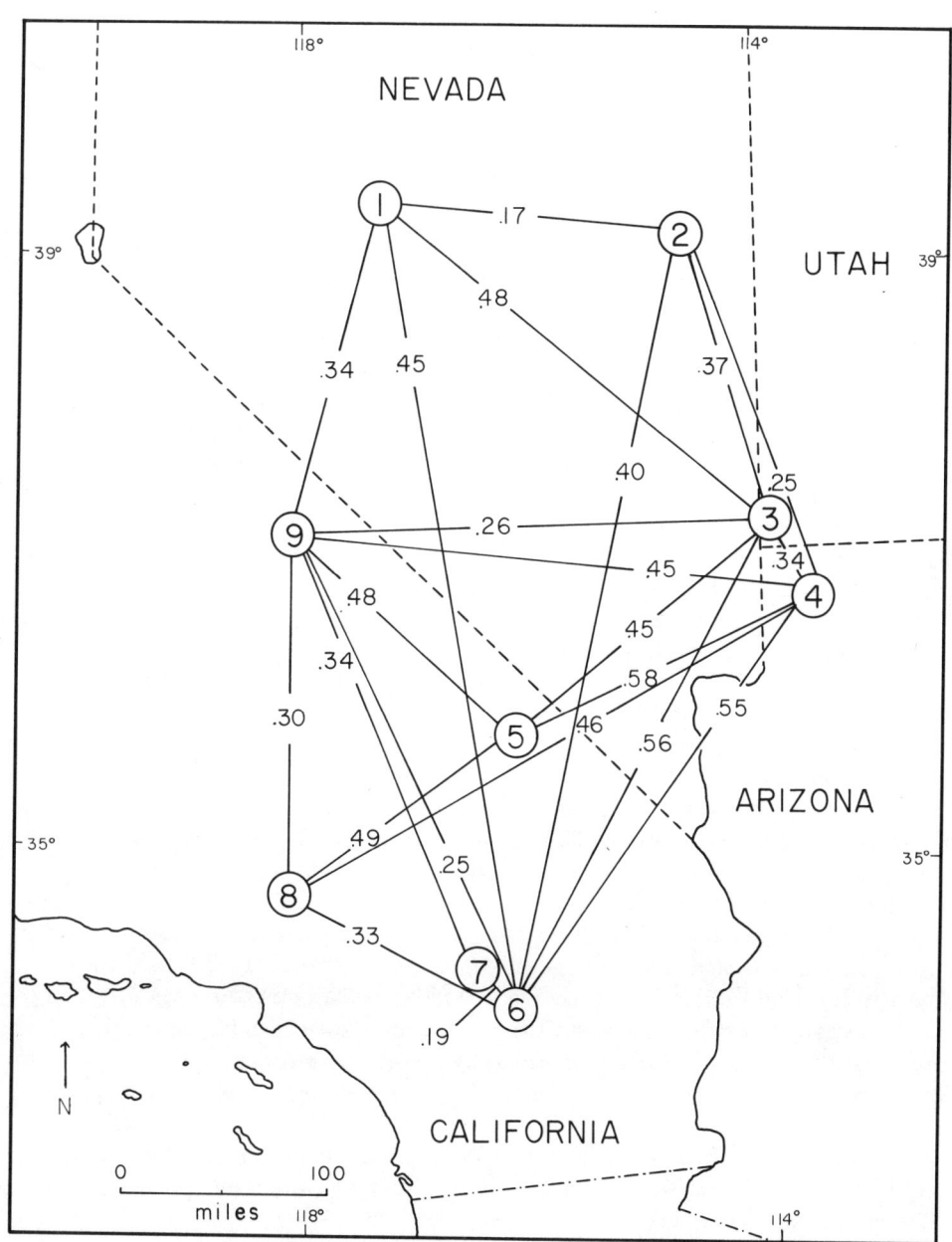

NEI DISTANCE BETWEEN POPULATIONS OF *DIPODOMYS MICROPS*

FIG. 7. Nei distances between populations of *Dipodomys microps*. Exact location of sample populations is indicated in figure 1.

morphological, karyotypic, and biochemical variation. A certain amount of quantifiable variation has been documented in every character set except the morphology of the lower incisors. The most striking dissimilarity between any of the populations surveyed is that of the karyotypic distinctiveness of the Joshua Tree National Monument population. This population alone possesses a karyotype resembling that of the broad-faced *heermanni* subgroup. Evidence seems strong (Kenagy, 1973b) that the chisel-shaped lower incisors of *D. microps* represent an adaptation for *Atriplex* foraging. Since the Joshua Tree population occupies an area devoid of *A. confertifolia*, but possesses the chisel-shaped lower incisors, I propose that this highland population: (1) is a recent invader to these mountains; (2) has affinities with the southern populations of *D. m. occidentalis* (based on cranial morphology, fig. 3); and (3) has a karyotypic difference which represents a derived rather than an ancestral condition for the species. The Yucca Valley population represents an intermediate situation, retaining the common *D. microps* karyotype but living in the blackbush zone of an adjacent desert mountain range. The biochemical identity of these two populations provides the strongest support for this hypothesis (table 6), and argues against any genetic separation between the two chromosomal forms. The alternative hypothesis, that the Joshua Tree karyotype is primitive for the species, would require a more recent evolution of the biarmed karyotype found throughout the remainder of the range. One would then expect to find relict populations with Joshua Tree-like karyotypes in peripheral populations occupying ancestral (=non-*Atriplex*) habitats. Specimens from such areas have been examined (San Bernardino Mountains, Kingston Range, Beaverdam Mountains, Virgin Mountains) and only the biarmed karyotype has been found. It follows that the superficial similarity between the Joshua Tree karyotype and that of the broad-faced species (Csuti, 1971; Stock, 1974) represents convergence in karyotypic evolution.

Cranial morphology, bacular dimensions, kidney anatomy, and protein electrophoretic data all indicate populations of *D. microps* found in northwestern Arizona are genetically distinct from those sampled in eastern California and western Nevada. It is probable, therefore, that the ecologic differences between these localities reflect some degree of ecological race formation. However, data from cranial and biochemical sources indicate that the observed geographic differences are clinal in nature. In both the southeastern and southwestern parts of its range, closely related adjacent populations of *D. microps* occur in different habitats (present study; Hardy, 1945), whereas more distantly related populations can be found occupying similar habitats. Differences detected in food niche or adaptive strategy among these populations may, therefore, be explained by non-genetic mechanisms as well as by genetic adaptation. Since these two modes of adaptation have been shown to be supportive rather than mutually exclusive (Heslop-Harrison, 1964), it is likely that a combination of genetic and non-genetic mechanisms accounts for differences in realized niche within this set of conspecific populations. The clinal nature of the differences within the species suggests that some type of direct response to habitat may play a role in determining different food niches and adaptive strategies among populations of the species. The following section will examine differences in adaptive strategy among these populations through field and laboratory investigations.

ADAPTATION FOR LIFE IN TWO HABITATS

Few species of wide distribution are so specialized that their community relations may be completely described by studies on a single population. Vaughan (1967), for example, calls attention to habitat-related variation in the food habits of *Thomomys talpoides*. This species may consume 50% prickly pear cactus in shortgrass prairie, but 93% forbs in mountain meadows. Definition of the role this species plays in community structure would be accordingly difficult. I will attempt to document similar adaptive variation in *Dipodomys microps* from two different communities. By investigating the mechanisms of adaptation facilitating this ecological polymorphism, the plasticity of the species' role in differing communities can be better appreciated.

STUDY SITES

In order to survey the spectrum of habitat types occupied by *D. microps,* several field trips were undertaken prior to selection of permanent study areas. The results of these surveys indicated that *D. microps* occurred in abundance only in two plant associations: desert valleys dominated by *Atriplex confertifolia,* and desert uplands with a *Coleogyne ramosissima* component. My experience indicates that statements in the literature placing *D. microps* in the sagebrush community apply to areas where there are small islands of *Atriplex* within the sagebrush zone. Only once, near an abandoned alfalfa field at Breen Creek, 7000 ft., Nye Co., Nevada, was *D. microps* found in a pure stand of Great Basin sagebrush. Here only one specimen was captured despite repeated trapping. All other occurrences of the species above the *Atriplex* zone were in areas dominated by *Coleogyne*. Two permanent study areas were chosen to represent the two habitats typical of the species.

Owens Valley.—4000 ft., Inyo Co., California; latitude 37°10'–37°25' N, longitude 118°20' W. To confirm Kenagy's (1972, 1973a, b) results and to provide a data base for comparisons with animals from non-*Atriplex* habitats to the southeast, four study sites were selected in the northern Owens Valley. Most effort was spent in an area 2 mi. E Big Pine (plate 2a). This site supports a moderately dense population of *D. microps* (see table 9) upon which in part Kenagy (1973b) bases his remarks on the foraging habits of the species.

The type locality of the species, near Lone Pine, was visited and ten topotypes were secured. Here the soil is rockier than at Big Pine and the site is slightly elevated above the valley floor. The vegetation at Lone Pine is similar to that at Big Pine but lacks a greasewood (*Sarcobatus*) component. A third area, similar in physiognomy to the type locality, was selected for comparative population sampling 1 mi. E White Mountain Research Station,

Bishop, California. Finally, a fourth site was chosen on the valley floor near Laws (20 miles north of Big Pine) from which specimens were removed for food habit studies. *Atriplex confertifolia* was the dominant plant at all of these sites. With the exception of the Lone Pine locality, all sites were on the east side of the Owens River, and were part of a continuous band of saltbush across the floor of the Owens Valley. While minor differences in plant composition were observed, there was no apparent barrier to gene flow among the populations sampled. These study sites are collectively referred to as *Owens Valley*, and represent the sample of *D. microps* from the *Atriplex* zone.

Wolf Hole.—10 mi. N Wolf Hole, Mohave Co., Arizona; latitude 36°53' N, longitude 113°33' W; 3800 ft. A second study area was selected on the eastern slopes of the Virgin Mountains of northwestern Arizona (plate 2b), in the blackbush zone near the type locality for *Dipodomys microps celsus* Goldman, 6 mi. N Wolf Hole (Goldman, 1924). Although there is some floristic variation between the Wolf Hole site and other southern mountain locations for the species (Kingston Range, Beaverdam Mountains, San Bernardino Mountains, and Little San Bernardino Mountains), the presence of blackbush seems to be indicative of *D. microps*. Beatley (1976a, b) also found *D. microps* closely associated with blackbush. This site is referred to as *Wolf Hole*.

CLIMATE

Owens Valley.—United States Weather Bureau (1964) records for Bishop Airport present an overview of the climatic conditions in the northern Owens Valley. These data are summarized in table 7. The Owens Valley receives an average of 5.84 inches (14.8 cm) of rainfall each year. This agrees with the figure of 4.51 inches given as an average for saltbush areas by Billings (1949). The rainfall is concentrated in the winter months during most years. The average monthly precipitation for June, July, August, and September is under 0.13 inches (0.33 cm). The coldest month is January, with a mean daily maximum of 52.7°F (11.5°C) and a mean daily minimum of 20.9°F (-5°C). The warmest month is July, with a mean daily maximum of 94.8°F (35°C) and a mean daily minimum of 54.8°F (13°C).

Wolf Hole.—The closest recording weather station to this study area is located 20 miles north at Saint George, Utah, 2880 ft. Comparisons between the two study sites based on these weather data must be made with caution, since the study area is 920 ft. (280 m) higher and could be expected to have lower temperatures and higher precipitation. This is confirmed by the vegetational zonation between St. George and the study area. At the Utah-Arizona border (2700 ft.), 10 miles south of St. George, cresote bush and *Atriplex confertifolia* are common. As one climbs steadily to the study site from this point, one passes out of the creosote bush belt and *A. confertifolia* is lost as a component of the vegetation. Only an occasional creosote bush occurs at the study area, and a lone piñon pine grows within 300 m of the trapping area.

Weather records (U. S. Weather Bureau, 1965) for St. George, Utah, are summarized in table 7. During the coldest month, January, the mean daily maximum is 53.2°F (12°C) and the mean daily minimum is 24.1°F (-4°C). The warmest month is July, with a mean daily maximum of 101.1°F (38°C) and a mean daily minimum of 64.5°F (18°C). Rainfall is 8.13 inches (20.7 cm) in a normal year; and, significantly, is more evenly distributed throughout the year, no month falling below 0.24 inches (0.61 cm). The monthly average for the four summer months is 0.51 inches (1.30 cm), four times that of the Owens Valley. Since this study site is higher than St. George and should have a cooler, moister climate, the difference in potential water stress to the biota between the study areas should be even greater than is indicated by these weather data.

TABLE 7. SUMMARY OF 1951-60 WEATHER RECORDS
FOR BISHOP, CALIFORNIA, AND ST. GEORGE, UTAH

	Jan	Feb	Mar	Apr	May	Jun	Jul	Aug	Sept	Oct	Nov	Dec	Annual
Bishop													
Mean daily maximum temp.	52.7	57.2	63.4	72.2	78.5	87.8	94.8	92.6	86.7	75.9	64.0	55.3	
Mean daily minimum temp.	20.9	25.7	29.1	36.2	42.2	48.7	54.8	51.7	45.5	36.0	26.3	21.2	
Average precipitation	.99	.98	.55	.46	.20	.09	.12	.12	.19	.43	.53	1.18	5.84
St. George													
Mean daily maximum temp.	53.2	59.1	67.2	76.4	85.4	95.8	101.1	99.0	92.5	79.8	64.9	53.8	
Mean daily minimum temp.	24.1	29.0	34.5	41.6	49.0	56.8	64.5	63.2	53.1	41.4	30.0	24.4	
Average precipitation	.98	1.03	.91	.48	.39	.24	.60	.61	.60	.68	.58	1.03	8.13

Temperatures are recorded in degrees Farenheit.
Precipitation is presented in inches.

PLANT COMMUNITIES

Quantification of the vegetation differences between the two study areas was undertaken to assess the availability and importance of potential forage species. Shrubs were censused using a 50 m transect line (Bauer, 1936, 1943). Percentage of shrub cover was estimated from 500 m of modified line intercept data (table 8). Herbaceous vegetation (forbs and grasses) was sampled with a 0.1 m² rectangular quadrat dropped randomly at 100 spots in each study area, following the method of Beatley (1976b). Herbs and grasses were scored as being in a quadrat if they were rooted within its borders (table 8).

Several major differences were observed between the two sites. The Wolf Hole site had a higher percentage of shrub cover, 24% as opposed to 19% in the Owens Valley, and a higher Shannon-Wiener diversity index, H', among shrub species (Shannon and Weaver, 1949). Grasses formed an important part of the plant community at Wolf Hole, with an average of 10.8 individuals per 0.1 m² quadrat. In contrast, grasses were almost absent from the *Atriplex* community of the Owens Valley. The only grass species present on the study area during vegetational sampling was rice grass (*Oryzopsis hymenoides*). No specimens of *Oryzopsis* were encountered in the random sampling of herbaceous vegetation described above. To

TABLE 8. COMPOSITION OF PLANT COMMUNITIES AT PERMANENT STUDY SITES

Owens Valley—4 mi. E Bishop, Inyo Co., California		
A. Shrubs	Species	Percent coverage
	open ground	80.79
	Atriplex confertifolia	11.19
	Atriplex polycarpa	3.60
	Dalea fremontii	1.17
	Menodora spinescens	1.21
	Lycium andersoni	.60
	Tetradymia axillaris	.10
	unknown 1	.10
	Shrub species diversity = 1.19	
B. Herbs	Density = 3.12/0.1 m², primarily *Eriogonum deflexum*	
Grasses	Density = 0.0023/0.1 m², *Oryzopsis hymenoides*	

Wolf Hole—10 mi. N Wolf Hole, Mohave Co., Arizona		
A. Shrubs	Species	Percent coverage
	open ground	76.33
	Yucca baccata	6.26
	Gutierrezia microcephala	5.33
	Lycium andersonii	4.87
	Coleogyne ramosissima	3.71
	Ephedra sp.	1.62
	Lotus sp.	1.16
	Tetradymia axillaris	.69
	Shrub species diversity = 1.76	
B. Herbs	*Erodium cicutarium, Lepidium fremontii* (presence inferred from burrow contents)	
Grasses	Density = 10.75/0.1 m². The following species were identified, in order of decreasing frequency: *Bromus rubens, Sitanion hystrix, Vulpia* (=*Festuca*) *sp., Hordeum sp.*	

estimate its frequency, the study area was marked off in a 10 x 10 m grid and all plants within a 100 m² area were counted. An average of 2.3 plants of *Oryzopsis* per 100 m² was calculated from ten such samples. Other varieties of grass were, however, abundant in areas grazed by cattle, where *Atriplex* was replaced by rabbit brush (*Chrysothamnus*); *Dipodomys microps* did not occur in areas of grazing disturbance that were sampled.

Not all species of grass were identified at Wolf Hole, but a majority of individuals were *Bromus rubens,* an introduced European annual. *Sitanion hystrix* was also common, and a *Vulpia (Festuca)* was present. Grasses found on the Wolf Hole study area are in part the result of introduction of European annuals associated with long-term cattle ranching in the area. Hardy (1945) reported accumulations (caches) of *Bromus rubens* seeds (following previous studies of heteromyid rodent food habits, the term *seed* will be used to refer to the caryopsis or grain of grasses) in burrows of *D. microps* at a site 41 km away. Seeds persist for years in desert environments and represent an abundant resource for species adapted for their use (Reichman, 1975; Nelson and Chew, 1977). Since grass seed production is low in the Owens Valley study area, the abundance of this potential resource at Wolf Hole must be considered as a factor shaping resource use and population biology of the small mammal community.

FAUNAL COMMUNITIES

Since interactions among members of the small mammal community are of potential importance in defining the niche shape of a species, a census of the small nocturnal mammals present at each study site was undertaken. At each locality a one hectare (100 m square) study grid was laid out in an undisturbed area lacking habitat disruptions such as rock outcrops or desert washes. Trapping stations were arrayed in a 10 x 10 m grid. Capture-mark-recapture trapping was carried out on two consecutive nights on three occasions at each site. During the first round of trapping an ear punch was used to mark animals, but in the following periods individually numbered ear tags ("fingerling" tags) were placed on all captured animals. Trapping was conducted with 3 x 3½ x 9 inch (7.6 x 8.9 x 22.9 cm) folding Sherman live traps baited with commercial wild bird seed. A Lincoln Index (Lincoln, 1930) was calculated for each mammal species captured. When recapture data were inadequate for calculation of this estimate, a minimum estimate was supplied for the species involved (total number of different individuals captured). Smith (1968) has compared different methods of estimating population density of small mammals. While the Lincoln Index has several theoretical disadvantages, in most cases it yields results comparable with other estimators of population density. Its reliability varies with species and sex, but since both study areas were surveyed with the same methods, comparisons made between them should reflect relative densities. Individuals of *D. microps* were readily recaptured; in four out of six trapping periods, over 90% of the animals caught on the second night of trapping were recaptures. With such high trapping success and so few new captures, my confidence in the accuracy of the technique, at least for this species, is high.

Minimum estimates for the relative population size of small mammal species captured on each study site are presented in table 9. Rodent density was twice as high at the Wolf Hole site, although the density of *D. microps* was approximately the same on the two study grids. The greater density of cricetid rodents at Wolf Hole accounted for most of this difference. This is likely a direct result of increased cover and diversity of vegetation at this site. The presence of *Yucca* at Wolf Hole was especially important to *Neotoma lepida*, providing both cover and sustenance. *Dipodomys merriami* was present in low numbers on the Wolf Hole

TABLE 9. SMALL MAMMAL COMMUNITY COMPOSITION AS DETERMINED BY
CAPTURE-MARK-RECAPTURE SAMPLING ON ONE HECTARE STUDY PLOTS IN TWO COMMUNITIES*

Species	Owens Valley September 27-28 1975	October 18-19 1975	July 8-9 1976	$\bar{x}$	Relative frequency	Wolf Hole September 20-21 1975	October 25-26 1975	September 28-29 1976	$\bar{x}$	Relative frequency
Dipodomys microps	13	12	7	11	.44	10	19	8	12	.24
Dipodomys merriami	7	3	4	5	.20	1	2	1	1	.02
Dipodomys deserti	1	1	–	1	.04					
Perognathus longimembris	2	–	2	2	.08	–	–	2	2	.04
Perognathus penicillatus						–	–	2	2	.04
Perognathus parvus	–	–	3	3	.12	7	6	–	7	.14
Peromyscus crinitus						18	12	1	10	.20
Peromyscus maniculatus	1	1	–	1	.04					
Onychomys torridus	2	2	–	2	.08	1	–	6	4	.08
Neotoma lepida						14	8	14	12	.24
Total				25	1.00				50	1.00
Species Diversity Index (H′)				1.60					1.82	

*Numbers are minimum estimates of animals present on the grid. Figures are summed for all trapping periods to obtain means. Only non-zero estimates are used in this calculation, so as not to underestimate rare species of those absent for physiological reasons (i.e., torpor).

study grid; however, in adjacent areas of human disturbance it occurred at higher densities, often being trapped as frequently as *D. microps*. The topography of this locality resulted in far greater patchiness than that seen in the Owens Valley.

Intensive trapping in and around the study grids on other occasions indicated that the distribution of visible rodent burrows differed between the sites. Only occasionally was a burrow entrance easily visible at the Owens Valley site, and trapping success seemed little influenced by placement of traps in proximity to those burrow entrances that were detectable. At Wolf Hole, conspicuous mounds were present, often with 12 to 24 entrances. This is similar to the situation described by Hardy (1949) in the nearby Beaverdam Mountains. Trapping at these mounds was usually successful, often yielding individuals of more than one species. Although no positive evidence was gathered to identify the resident of any particular burrow complex, repeated instances of a female and several juvenile *D. microps,* or of a female and two males of this species at one mound indicated these burrow complexes were typically occupied by *D. microps*. Hardy (1945) also concluded these mounds were indicative of *D. microps*.

On several occasions *D. merriami* were captured at the entrances to a burrow labyrinth during the same trap night as one or more *D. microps*. While the baited traps may have drawn the animals to the location of the mound, their capture suggests that *D. merriami* will visit *D. microps* mounds while foraging. Vorhies and Taylor (1922) report instances of suspected pilfering of seed stores by *D. merriami* at *D. spectabilis* mounds. Large caches of seed are present in *D. microps* burrows in this region (see Hardy, 1945; following section). Captures of *D. merriami* at entrances to *D. microps* burrows may result from seed-pilfering by the former species.

Dipodomys microps occurs at the same density and has many of the same potential competitors at both study areas. There is a substantial granivorous component to the small mammal community at Wolf Hole. The fact that *D. microps* successfully exploits the seed-eating niche at Wolf Hole suggests differences in resource base, rather than interspecific interactions, are responsible for geographic differences in realized niche within the species.

FOOD HABITS

Through a combination of field observation of foraging behavior, feeding trials, and examination of the contents of nine burrow systems, Kenagy (1973b) concluded that the population of *D. microps* he studied in the Owens Valley fed primarily if not exclusively on *Atriplex confertifolia* leaves. Beatley (1976a) pointed out that reliance by *D. microps* on succulent leaves as a food or water source in southern Nevada would not be possible, due to the deciduous nature of the perennial shrubs in that region. A survey of the literature indicates that while the phytophagous habit of *D. microps* has been documented throughout the central and northern parts of its range, granivory is indicated along the southern margin of the species' distribution.

Fautin (1946:281) reported that *Atriplex* leaves formed the major food source for *D. microps* and that captive individuals "readily stripped the leaves from shadscale stems and preferred them to any other vegetation." Johnson (1961) reported on the food habits of *D. microps* in southern Idaho and found the species relied heavily on shadscale leaves for food, but also found grass seeds taken to some extent in the late summer. He also notes a limited amount of geographic variation in diet, the frequency of *Atriplex* leaves versus grass seeds in cheek pouches being 54% to 3% respectively, in the Raft River Valley; but 32% to 58% in the Elmore Desert. In further work (Larrison and Johnson, 1973) the importance of leaves in the diet of *D. microps* is confirmed. Warnock and Grundman (1963) found both shadscale leaves and grass seeds in *D. microps* stomachs in Utah, as did Anderson and Allred (1964) in burrows of *D. microps* at the Nevada Test Site. Hardy (1945, 1949) excavated *D. microps* burrows in southern Utah and reported finding large caches of seeds but no *Atriplex* leaves.

In order to document variation in diet present between the *D. microps* populations of the Owens Valley and Wolf Hole, I undertook a study of food habits, relying primarily on stomach content information gathered from snap-trapped specimens. Samples of plant material from cheek pouches of snap-trapped specimens were saved for identification. On a single occasion in the Owens Valley I observed an animal released from a live trap climb into an *Atriplex* bush and begin eating the leaves. In addition to cheek pouch and stomach content data, six burrow systems were excavated at each site and the contents of food caches were sampled.

Stomach contents were analyzed by microscopic procedures outlined by Baumgartner and Martin (1939) and Hansson (1970). Stomachs from the specimens taken at the Owens Valley site were removed immediately after capture and transferred to 70% ethyl alcohol. Specimens from Wolf Hole were frozen on dry ice in the field and transported back to the laboratory. Here the animals were partly thawed and the stomachs were removed to 70% ethyl alcohol. Hannson (1970) found neither freezing nor storage in alcohol appreciably affected the characters used in micro-analysis of the contents.

The total contents of a stomach were boiled for three minutes in Hertwig's Solution (Baumgartner and Martin, 1939) to clear intracellular material and were then washed on a 65 mesh Tyler Standard Screen. Agitation during the washing process insured complete mixing of the contents. The specimen was then stained for five minutes in a solution of Delafield's hematoxylin and washed again in running water. Twenty random fields were examined at 125x magnification. Empty fields or those with unidentifiable fragments were not scored. Relative frequency of occurrence was calculated for each food item after the method presented by Reichman (1975). Although this method of quantification may tend to overestimate rare food items (Hansson, 1970), Sparks and Malechek (1968) document its overall accuracy.

Plant reference material was collected in the field during trapping periods. Additional reference material was taken from excavated burrow systems at which *D. microps* had been captured. Dried plant reference material was ground in a Wiley mill over a 40 mesh screen, then treated identically to stomach content material. This treatment resulted in particle sizes that were comparable in unknown and reference material. Black and white prints of photomicrographs showing characteristic structures in reference material were prepared to aid in scoring stomach content slides. In some instances specific identification of stomach content fragments was impossible; however general structure was usually distinct enough to allow classification into categories such as leaf material, seed coat (monocot), or seed coat (dicot).

Cheek pouch contents of three Wolf Hole specimens captured 3-4 May 1976 contain some leafy material, primarily blackbush leaves, but also some grass seeds and spikes (*Bromus rubens*). An individual live-trapped on 23 March 1975 in similar habitat in Joshua Tree National Monument was carrying forb clippings in its cheek pouches. Two specimens taken in the summer from the Owens Valley carried *Atriplex, Lycium,* and *Sarcobatus* leaves.

Burrow contents from the Owens Valley contained *Atriplex* leaves, leaf shavings, and bracts, the latter usually smaller than the average size seen on plants in the vicinity, and some *Sarcobatus* leaves. Excavation of burrows at Wolf Hole often unearthed large stores of grass seeds (*Bromus rubens, Hordeum sp., Vulpia* [*Festuca*] *sp.*) sometimes mixed with smaller quantities of other seeds (*Erodium cicutarium, Lotus sp., Lepidium fremontii*), but never any leafy material. Seeds of *Bromus rubens, Coleogyne ramosissima,* and *Thamnosma montana* were found in two burrow systems excavated in the Beaverdam Mountains.

Results of stomach content micro-analysis are presented in table 10. Samples from the Owens Valley population reveal a predominance of *Atriplex confertifolia* leaves in the diet, confirming the suggestion of Kenagy (1973b). Other dietary items detected were leaves of shrubs such as *Lycium* and *Dalea* and an occasional seed coat. Herbaceous vegetation at this site consisted almost entirely of *Eriogonum deflexum,* and the apparent absence of grass seed in stomach contents may reflect the low availability of this potential food item as well as a preference for *Atriplex. Atriplex confertifolia* was the most common shrub in the area (table 8), accounting for 62% of the total shrub cover. Its occurrence in the diet with a relative frequency of 80% may indicate a relationship between availability and use; however, the size of the sample does not allow definitive conclusions.

Samples from Wolf Hole were taken in both spring and fall (table 10). Far more green vegetation is present in the diet in the spring sample. Since blackbush (the most common leaf in the diet) is partly or completely deciduous during most years (Beatley, 1976b), the diet appears to reflect changing seasonal availability of food resources. Flake (1973) and Alcoze and Zimmerman (1973) have shown seasonal changes in percentages of seed and greenery in the diet of *D. ordii.* The greater proportion of green vegetation in the spring diet coincides with breeding and lactation. Beatley (1969), Bradley and Mauer (1971), and Soholt (1977) discuss the correlation between increased availability of succulent vegetation and breeding in *D. merriami.* Although some species of *Dipodomys* may be able to maintain weight on dry diets (Schmidt-Nielsen, K., 1964), the demands of lactation require access to succulent vegetation

TABLE 10. RESULTS OF STOMACH CONTENTS ANALYSIS

Owens Valley July-August 1976 n = 12		Wolf Hole May 1976 n = 4		Wolf Hole September 1976 n = 6	
Species	RF	Species	RF	Species	RF
Atriplex leaf	80.3%	blackbush leaf	29.7%	grass seed coat	60.9%
mallow flower	10.6%	*Lycium* leaf	14.3%	grass seed 1	5.0%
Dalea leaf	5.6%	filaree leaf	3.6%	*Gutierrezia* leaf, flower	14.2%
filaree leaf	.4%	*Lotus* leaf	9.5%	blackbush leaf	19.9%
Lycium leaf	2.7%	rosette leaf	2.4%		
unknown seed	.4%	mallow flower	1.2%		
		unknown leaf	2.4%		
		grass seed 1	10.7%		
		grass seed 2	3.6%		
		grass seed 3	1.2%		
		grass seed 4	15.5%		
		unknown seed	4.7%		
Total *Atriplex* leaf	80.3%	Total leaf	64.3%	Total leaf	34.1%
Total other leaf	19.3%	Total seed	35.7%	Total seed	65.9%
Total seed	.4%				
Plant species/stomach	2.2	Plant species/stomach	6.5	Plant species/stomach	2.7

RF = relative frequency.

x 12-7/8 x 6-5/8 inch (38 x 33 x 17 cm) polyethylene cages lined with a layer of sand to allow sand-bathing necessary to maintain pelage quality. No nesting material was provided in order to eliminate individual differences in the use of such material. Temperature in animal rooms varied within the limits described for each experiment in the following sections. When native vegetation was provided, it was supplied in excess (i.e., leaf bearing branches and twigs totaling ca. 500 g) and changed for fresh material each evening. These experiments were conducted over the course of several years and modifications to the later experiments were made as indicated by results obtained in earlier ones. For this reason the specific design, conditions, and results of each experiment will be presented below in chronological order.

Monitoring changes in body weight is a simple and convenient method of quantifying an animal's response to variations in diet or moisture supply. Kenagy (1973b), Vaughan (1967), MacMillen (1964), Church (1969), and others have used this method extensively in their analyses of food and water requirements of various rodents. Despite the utility of the technique, certain problems are encountered in data presentation and analysis which will be discussed here as a precursor to the presentation of results.

Lindeborg (1952) noted that the response of specimens to water restriction is not linear. Rate of water loss is often greatest during the initial period, followed by a period of stabilization or slow weight reduction. Among specimens that die, this rate again accelerates immediately prior to death. Since weights of a single specimen in successive periods are not independent of one another, the assumptions of independence required for calculating regression lines are not met. Several strategies have been used to circumvent this problem. Mares (1975) merely plots mean percentage of initial body weight during the course of the experiment. Kenagy (1973b) and Johnson and Ohmart (1973) use the same approach, but record sample size at each interval, which diminishes with stress-related mortality. As one might predict, the highest mortality is observed in specimens which have lost the most weight. Since the death of a light individual removes a low value from the calculations, the group average may rise in the succeeding interval, even if the trend for the survivors continues downward. Vaughan (1967) handles this problem by plotting two averages, one for animals that lived through the experiment, another for animals that die. MacMillen and Christopher (1975) use average values of the entire group in their presentation, but terminate the curve before the first mortality occurs, thereby avoiding this problem. Lindeborg (1952) and MacMillen (1964) plot averaged weight indices calculated from a formula which compensates for deaths by assuming that all animals survive to the end of the experiment. This method admittedly yields artificially low average weight values in the latter stages of the trial, but relative comparisons may still be made.

During the course of my experiments, varying degrees of tolerance to dietary regimes were observed and there were considerable differences in individual response. I concluded that averaging the weights of all subjects did not necessarily reflect the pattern of response to a given experimental condition. For example, it is certainly misleading to combine results for a specimen that died in one week with one that survived for five weeks. Lindeborg (1952:19) concluded that "the best criterion for evaluating the effect of reduced water ration was the length of time a mouse can survive it." Since I was measuring the ability to use various food items (e.g., dry seed, *Atriplex* leaves, blackbush leaves), I took the ability to survive the test conditions coupled with ability to maintain weight (not all survivors maintain weight equally well) as indices to be used in the statistical comparisons of my feeding trials.

Test conditions varied considerably, depending on previous treatment of test subjects and environmental conditions in the animal facilities. Although trends among similar experiments performed under different conditions are considered, results are analyzed for statistically significant differences only when test runs were identical in all respects other than the variable under consideration. Functionally this meant comparing only simultaneous feeding trials. For graphic presentation, the percentage of initial body weight throughout an experiment is illustrated on the same figure for each specimen. This allows assessment of individual variation within the group, displays overall trends, and avoids the biases in presentation discussed above.

Comparisons between experiments are made using the Wilcoxon Two-Sample Test (Sokal and Rohlf, 1969). Performance data of all individuals are ordered as if coming from a single sample and each individual is assigned a rank depending on length of survival. In cases where survival time was the same, percentage of original weight on the last day is used as an additional criterion. If ties still exist, rank is divided among the tied individuals. Sums of rank for each of the two groups being compared are then calculated and the resulting U-statistic is compared with tables of the Mann-Whitney U-statistic to determine the level of significance of any difference observed.

Experiment I

Informal experiments conducted in the spring of 1973 with specimens from an *Atriplex* community near Lancaster, Los Angeles Co., California, suggested that although *Atriplex* leaves were used as a food item by members of this population, seeds and other types of leaves were also eaten and that survival on dry seed diets may be influenced by the amount of succulent vegetation available during early development. To test the response of a *Coleogyne* zone population of *D. microps* to a dry seed diet, a series of eight specimens was collected at Wolf Hole between 14 August and 19 September, 1973. Commerical wild bird mix was provided *ad libitum*, but no succulent vegetation or water was given. Animals were maintained at Berkeley in a room with natural lighting whose temperature fluctuated between 70-80°F (21-27°C) and whose relative humidity ranged between 50-60%. Each specimen was weighed to the nearest one-half gram daily or on alternate days with a 100 g Pesola scale and a plastic holding bag of known weight.

After losing weight during the first week, most specimens were able to regain weight without access to free water or succulent vegetation. The average weight of survivors (seven of

TABLE 11. EXPERIMENT I: WEIGHT MAINTENANCE AND SURVIVAL OF FALL-CAUGHT WOLF HOLE ADULT *DIPODOMYS MICROPS* ON DRY SEED DIETS AT BERKELEY
(Test duration, 33 days)

Specimen number	Days survived	Percent original weight
100	33	103
101	33	96
103	33	96
104	33	100
105	26	89
106	33	97
107	33	107
108	33	93
		$\bar{x}$ = 98 (99)*

*Mean weight of surviving specimens is given in parentheses.

eight) at the end of 38 days was 99% of original body weight (table 11). The response of these eight Wolf Hole animals to dry seed diet indicated this population of *D. microps* was adapted to withstand periods of moisture deprivation. These results differ from those reported by Kenagy (1973b) for a sample of seven *D. microps* from the Owens Valley and confirm the presence of significant physiological variation in the species, as suggested by the presence of seed caches and the absence of *Atriplex* at Wolf Hole.

Experiment II

The results of Experiment I indicated that comparative population studies would be of interest. In the late fall of 1973 I collected additional specimens from Wolf Hole and transported these to the Owens Valley Laboratory of the University of California's White Mountain Research Station, 4 mi. E Bishop, Inyo Co., California. A comparative sample of *D. microps* from the Owens Valley was then secured. Specimens were housed in the station's main animal room, which consisted of a windowless 15 x 15 ft. room on a 12-hour light cycle. Temperature was maintained by an electrically-operated window-type heat exchanger installed in one wall of the building which served both heating and cooling needs. Temperature ranged between 68-80°F (20-27°C). No hygrometer was available; however ambient relative humidities in the Bishop area are under 20% on days without precipitation. Ages of the test subjects were not known; however, all were of adult weight and presumably the youngest had been born the previous spring, as fall breeding is not reported for *D. microps* (Hall, 1946; Kenagy, 1973a).

During this experiment, each study population was subdivided into three groups: control animals receiving wild bird mix and *ad libitum* lettuce; "seed-only" animals, receiving commercial wild bird mix (hereafter laboratory diets of "dry seed" or "seed" refer to commercial wild bird mix) but no source of moisture; and "*Atriplex*-only" animals, receiving about 500 g of fresh *A. confertifolia* foliage each day. *Atriplex* foliage provided in this and subsequent experiments was harvested from the field daily an hour before dusk to insure maximum palatability.

Owens Valley specimens fed *Atriplex*-only responded as well as control specimens, maintaining their weight at original levels, whereas animals given only dry seed lost weight rapidly (fig. 8). These results agree with those of Kenagy (1973b). Table 12 summarizes performance of Wolf Hole specimens under the various regimes. Animals on dry seed diets either maintained constant weight or tended to lose weight at a slow rate throughout the duration of the experiment. Those on control diets gained weight, and specimens fed an *Atriplex*-only diet (n=4) lost weight rapidly. Only a single specimen in this last group survived to day 15, and that one weighed only 77% of its initial weight.

This experiment serves to illustrate the different patterns of resource use among populations of *D. microps*. While Owens Valley specimens maintain weight on *Atriplex* leaves, those from Wolf Hole do not. Under the test conditions, neither population sample was able to maintain weight on a dry seed diet. However half of the individuals from Wolf Hole did maintain weight on this regime, whereas both Owens Valley specimens lost weight. Nevertheless, weight maintenance of Wolf Hole specimens on a seed-only regime was below that of the Wolf Hole sample tested in Berkeley the previous month. The lower atmospheric moisture content in the Owens Valley facility may be partly responsible for this result. The Schmidt-Nielsens (1950) report the relative humidity of kangaroo rat burrows as 35% for *D. spectabilis* (range 18-62%) and about 40% for *D. merriami* (range 13-91%), although the latter data are based on relatively few observations. For *Dipodomys* species whose water conservation abilities are

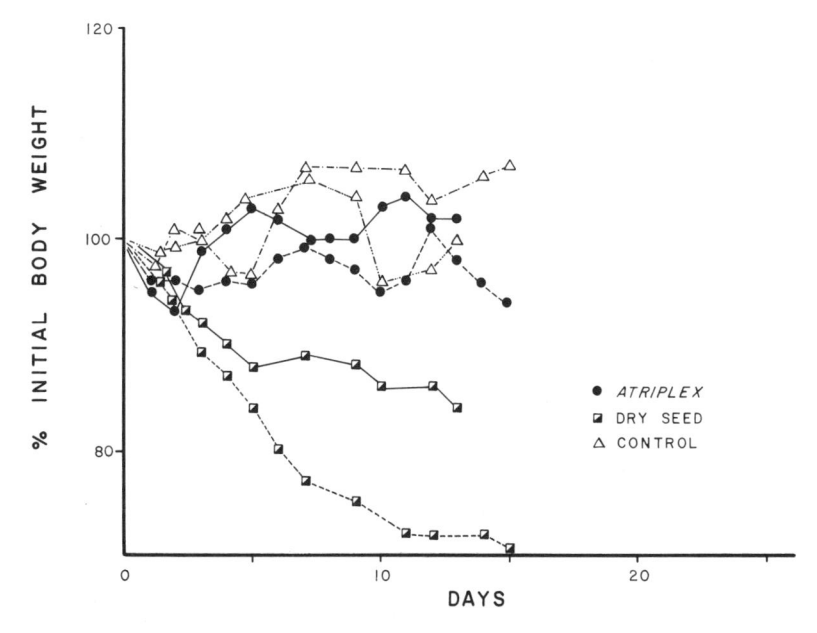

OWENS VALLEY ADULTS — *ATRIPLEX*, DRY SEED, CONTROL DIETS

FIG. 8. Experiment II: Weight maintenance of six Owens Valley adults on *Atriplex* leaf, dry seed, and control (=dry seed and lettuce) diets at Bishop. Each line represents the record of a single individual.

marginal, such as *D. agilis* (Carpenter, 1966) or *D. venustus* (Church, 1969), weight maintenance during periods of moisture stress may depend on the animal's ability to spend much of its time in the humid environment of the burrow. It is possible that even in a xeric-adapted population of *D. microps* the atmospheric moisture content within the burrow is a critical factor during those seasons when succulent vegetation is unavailable.

While the results of this experiment further indicate a physiological and behavioral difference between the two populations, these data do not allow identification of the mechanisms contributing to these differences. Further experiments were therefore planned involving young raised under controlled conditions.

Experiment III

During the early spring of 1974 extensive field work was undertaken to secure larger samples of *Atriplex* and *Coleogyne* zone populations of *D. microps*. Female specimens thought to be pregnant on the basis of high body weight were identified in the field and given special attention (i.e., daily supplements of rolled oats and lettuce, ample nesting material). *Atriplex* community specimens were collected from the Owens Valley and from Smith Creek Valley, Lander Co., Nevada. Blackbush zone populations were represented by samples from Wolf Hole and from the Kingston Range, San Bernardino Co., California. Fifty-two adult and 11 young *Dipodomys* were used in this experiment. Young were born in the laboratory at Berkeley and maintained there until the oldest were four weeks of age, which is approximately the age of weaning (Lackey, 1967a). All specimens were then transported to the Owens Valley Laboratory of the White Mountain Research Station and installed in the main animal room. In an effort to raise the relative humidity in this room, I set out 20 water-filled pans, aver-

TABLE 12. EXPERIMENT II: WEIGHT MAINTENANCE AND SURVIVAL
OF WOLF HOLE ADULTS
(Test duration, 15 days)

Diet	Specimen number	Days survived	Percent original weight at termination
Control	100	15	122
	101	15	112
	103	15	103
	104	15	117
	135	15	111
	136	15	111
	137	15	123
	120	15	109
Dry seed	126	15	91
	127	15	101
	128	15	82
	129	15	100
	130	15	98
	131	15	88
	105	15	98
	107	15	91
	106	15	98
	108	15	85
Atriplex leaves	121	2	89
	122	14	77
	124	14	82
	125	15	77

Wilcoxon Two-Sample tests for differences in survival and terminal weight between groups: control vs. Atriplex—difference significant at $p = .05$; control vs. seed—difference significant at $p = .05$; seed vs. Atriplex—difference significant at $p = .05$.

aging 1200 cm² surface area. Relative humidity fluctuated between 20 and 30%, depending on outdoor weather conditions. Occasionally high winds would lower inside humidity to 10%.

Samples of adult animals were maintained on a variety of regimes commencing 1 June. Adults representing *Coleogyne* zone populations were fed: (1) control diets—seed and lettuce *ad libitum;* (2) *Atriplex* foliage only; (3) *Coleogyne* foliage only (to test whether these populations are leaf-eaters, using the dominant shrub in their habitat); and (4) dry seed only. Samples from *Atriplex* communities were tested on dry seed and on *Atriplex* diets. Since previous experiments indicated no difference between control and *Atriplex* responses in this population, and since this sample was smaller than that from the *Coleogyne* zone, the *Atriplex*-feeding segment of this population served as a control for the seed-only segment. Fautin (1946) suggested that *D. ordii* fed on *Atriplex* leaves. This species is sympatric with *D. microps* in the northern parts of the latter's range. Since interactions between these congeners could influence patterns of resource use in *D. microps,* I placed a sample of seven *D. ordii* on *Atriplex*-only diets to measure their ability to survive on a diet of saltbush leaves.

Following weaning, captive-born young were subjected to two early diets: seed and lettuce *ad libitum;* and limited amounts of seed plus *Atriplex* foliage *ad libitum.* Small amounts (5 g/day) of seed were given in combination with *Atriplex* during a three- to four-week postweaning period to supply nutritional requirements that may be lacking in a diet consisting solely of *Atriplex* leaves. Increase in weight is rapid in *Dipodomys* until two months of age, following which time the rate of growth slows (Lackey, 1967a). At approximately two months of age young animals from each of the two early treatment groups were tested for their ability to maintain weight on two dietary regimes: (1) a diet of *Atriplex* leaves; and (2) a dry seed diet. Since the area of origin of the young animals is known, any overriding genetic control of the physiological and behavioral abilities under investigation should be apparent. On the other hand, if developmental flexibility is responsible for the two ecological morphs of the species, and if laboratory conditions approximate field conditions well enough to direct development of the appropriate adaptive mechanisms, then early experience should be correlated with weight maintenance on the test diet, regardless of area of origin.

Adult animals. Table 13 summarizes the response of *Coleogyne* zone specimens to the various test diets. While specimens fed a control diet maintained weight during this experiment, a general downward trend in body weight was observed in specimens given a dry seed diet. Of the original sample of nine, only two animals survived to day 29. These results differ from previously conducted tests with this diet. During Experiment I, conducted at Berkeley, seven of eight Wolf Hole adults were able to maintain weight on dry seed diets. Moreover, the rate of weight loss observed in the present sample was greater than it was for those specimens that lost weight under similar conditons during Experiment II.

These results suggest that the combined effects of acclimation in the field and atmospheric moisture levels modify the ability of blackbush zone specimens to tolerate periods of water stress. The specimens used in Experiment I were captured on 21 July 1973, by which time natural vegetation would have lost much of its moisture content, and were tested under the high relative humidity conditions in the Berkeley animal room. Of the 10 animals used in Experiment II, four had also been used in Experiment I and the remaining six were captured on 27 September 1973, during the dryest period of the year at Wolf Hole. Terminal body weight was 93% of original weight for this sample of 10 animals. Although there was a range of response in this group, five specimens maintaining weight (99%) over the test period, and five losing weight (87%), I ascribe this difference to individual variation, since there was no correlation with the previous treatment given individuals. Experiment III, however, was carried out in the Owens Valley animal room, where relative humidity was lower than at Berkeley. The animals used in this experiment were either captured on trips in the spring of the year (four out of eight) or had been used in previous experiments and had been fed lettuce *ad libitum* over the winter. The final body weight of 59% of the initial figure for the lone survivor indicates these animals were completely unable to maintain weight on dry seed when abruptly shifted to this regime in the Owens Valley animal room, with its low atmospheric moisture. In view of the results of Experiment III, a repetition of a test demonstrating the ability of blackbush zone specimens to survive on dry seed diets was needed to confirm evidence of geographic variation in adaptive strategy among *D. microps* populations (see Experiment VI).

Results of *Atriplex* feeding trials with blackbush zone specimens are shown in figure 9. As previously indicated, most animals seemed unable to use these leaves as a food item and quickly lost weight. A single individual began producing leaf shavings after a short latent period during which weight was lost. This specimen regained lost weight, then stabilized at 87% of its initial weight for a three-week period, efficiently feeding on *Atriplex confertifolia* leaves. Although this response was observed in only a single adult specimen, it suggests that the potential for the complex behavior patterns involved in shaving *Atriplex* leaves exists

TABLE 13. EXPERIMENT III. WEIGHT MAINTENANCE AND SURVIVAL OF *COLEOGYNE* ZONE ADULT *DIPODOMYS MICROPS*
(Test duration, 45 days)

Diet	Specimen number	Days survived	Percent original weight at termination
Control	130	45	113
	185	45	120
	161	45	96
Dry seed	101	24	64
	106	13	66
	123	16	70
	136	16	66
	126	29	59
	151	29	60
	153	11	73
	165	21	56
	166	18	69
Atriplex leaves	156	35	67
	107	10	73
	132	10	77
	127	12	77
	162	3	85
	163	2	93
	164	6	77
Coleogyne leaves	96	4	85
	128	8	73
	154	8	73
	168	4	79
	160	8	78
	184	11	78
	152	21	69
	167	29	90

Wilcoxon Two-Sample tests for differences in survival and terminal weight between groups: control vs. *Atriplex*—difference significant at $p = .05$; control vs. dry seed—difference significant at $p = .05$; control vs. *Coleogyne*—difference significant at $p = .05$; *Coleogyne* vs. *Atriplex*—no significant difference.

in upland populations of *D. microps,* but that these patters are not readily expressed in adult specimens from this zone. If leaf-shaving is inherent in blackbush populations, then either of two mechanisms may govern its expression: (1) early exposure to these leaves may modify development toward efficiency in leaf-handling and lack of such exposure may determine a course of development leading to efficient granivory—this modification may be incomplete in some individuals, accounting for the anomalous behavior of one individual in this experiment; (2) most non-*Atriplex* feeding adult *D. microps* may be induced to demonstrate this behavior pattern provided they have sufficient time to physiologically and behaviorally adjust to *Atriplex* as a novel food item. These mechanisms were investigated in Experiment V.

A final subset of the *Coleogyne* zone population was fed a diet of leaves and twigs of *Col-*

COLEOGYNE ZONE ADULTS, ATRIPLEX DIET

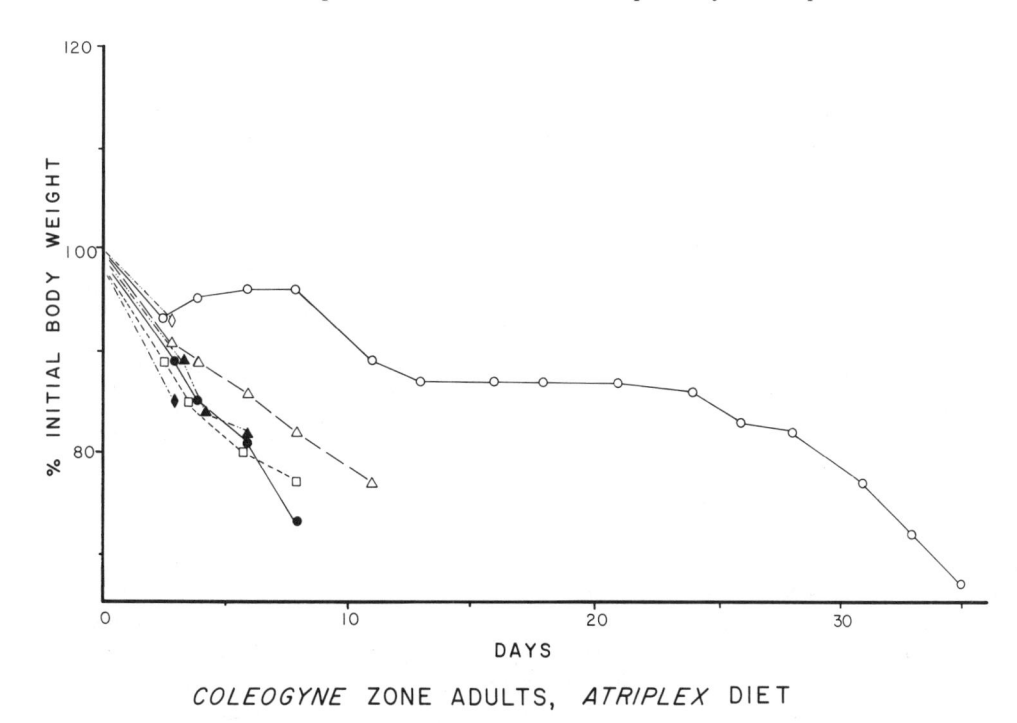

FIG. 9. Experiment III: Weight maintenance of seven *Coleogyne* zone adults on an *Atriplex* leaf diet at Bishop. Each line represents the record of a single individual.

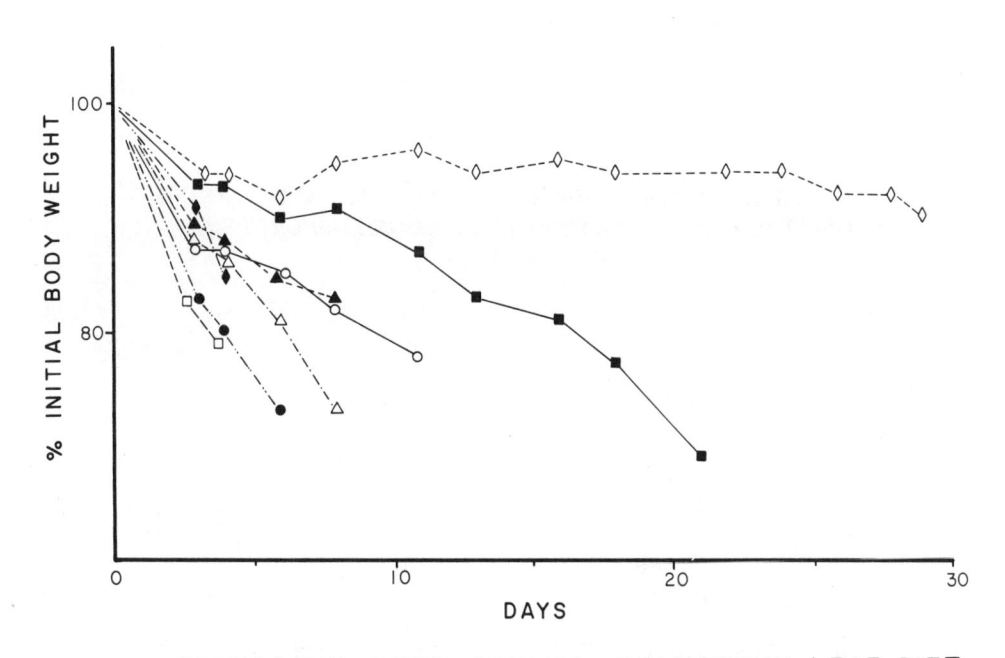

COLEOGYNE ZONE ADULTS, COLEOGYNE LEAF DIET

FIG. 10. Experiment III: Weight maintenance of eight *Coleogyne* zone adults on a diet of *Coleogyne* foliage at Bishop. Each line represents the record of a single individual.

eogyne ramosissima. The results (fig. 10) resemble those of the *Atriplex* feeding experiments in that 75% of the individuals quickly lost weight and died. However, two survived, one losing weight slowly for three weeks, the other maintaining weight at over 90% of original level for more than four weeks. Blackbush has small linear leaves that are not shaved but eaten *in toto.* The individual who survived longest also stripped bark off the twigs and consumed the rather large developing seeds still within the seed capsules. Blackbush seeds were found in burrow caches of *D. microps* in the Beaverdam Mountains of southwestern Utah. It is difficult to say how much nutritional value is contained in various parts of the plant, or which parts were most important to the individuals tested here, but the results indicate that the species can use foliage of this shrub for supplementary food and moisture when it is available.

Results of experiments with *Atriplex* habitat samples are presented in table 14. The ability to maintain weight on *Atriplex* or dry seed regimes paralleled that of Experiment II. Aside from an unexplained early death in the *Atriplex* diet subset, accompanied by very little weight loss, these animals maintained 100% of original body weight for a period of seven weeks on a diet of saltbush leaves. A subset fed a dry seed diet succumbed within two weeks.

Dipodomys ordii. Seven *D. ordii* were placed in cages with leaves of *Atriplex confertifolia* as the only food item. None shaved the leaves or consumed noticeable amounts of this foliage, and none survived longer than two weeks under these conditions. This suggests that saltbush leaves are unlikely to be a primary source of nutrition for the species. If interactions between *D. ordii* and *D. microps* do influence the realized niche of the latter, evidence suggests that they take some form other than competition for the use of the *Atriplex*-leaf resource.

Captive-born young. Young were divided into four groups receiving different treatments (table 15). The weight-maintenance curves of these young (fig. 11) may be summarized as follows: (1) young given seed and minimal lettuce in the post-weaning period were no better able to maintain weight on an all seed diet than any other group, regardless of their area of origin. The low humidity in the Bishop animal room may have precluded any *D. microps* from successfully maintaining weight on a dry seed diet, regardless of previous history; (2) young fed seed and lettuce during the post-weaning period were unable to use *Atriplex* leaves

TABLE 14. EXPERIMENT III. WEIGHT MAINTENANCE AND SURVIVAL
OF *ATRIPLEX*-HABITAT ADULT *DIPODOMYS MICROPS*
(Test duration, 47 days)

Diet	Specimen number	Days survived	Percent original weight at termination
Atriplex leaves	169	47	107
	170	47	97
	178	8	91
	183	47	103
Dry seed	180	8	71
	181	10	68
	182	13	60

Wilcoxon Two-Sample tests for differences in survival and terminal weight between groups: *Atriplex* leaves vs. Dry seed—no significant difference (lack of significant difference may be an artifact of small sample size—note difference in survival times and weights). Comparison with *Coleogyne* zone adults (table 13): *Atriplex* leaf subgroups—difference significant at $p = .05$; Dry seed subgroups—difference significant at $p = .05$.

TABLE 15. EXPERIMENT III. EXPERIMENTAL DESIGN AND RESULTS OF FEEDING TRIALS WITH CAPTIVE-BORN YOUNG
(Test duration, 16 days)

Locality of parental population	Early diet	Test diet	Specimen number	Days survived	Percent original weight at termination
Wolf Hole	seed + lettuce	dry seed	155a*	6	81
Owens Valley	seed + lettuce	dry seed	178a	8	77
Wolf Hole	seed + lettuce	*Atriplex*	157b	4	89
Owens Valley	seed + lettuce	*Atriplex*	178b	10	74
Kingston Range	seed + lettuce	*Atriplex*	167a	6	77
Wolf Hole	*Atriplex* + seed	*Atriplex*	156b	16	101
Wolf Hole	*Atriplex* + seed	*Atriplex*	157a	10	97
Kingston Range	*Atriplex* + seed	*Atriplex*	168a	16	100
Kingston Range	*Atriplex* + seed	*Atriplex*	168b	16	104
Wolf Hole	*Atriplex* + seed	dry seed	156a	6	89
Wolf Hole	*Atriplex* + seed	dry seed	158a	6	82

Wilcoxon Two-Sample test for differences in survival and terminal weight between groups: *Atriplex* early diet, *Atriplex* test diet vs. seed + lettuce early diet, *Atriplex* test diet—difference significant at $p = .05$. Other combinations too small to test using this procedure.
*Lower case letters following specimen numbers are used to identify offspring (e.g., 156a and 156b are captive-born offspring of specimen No. 156).

as a food item, even if they were offspring of *Atriplex*-feeding mothers; (3) young from *Coleogyne* zone populations given early exposure to *Atriplex* (with small seed supplements) do not maintain weight when placed on an all seed diet—same comments as for (1), above, apply; (4) young representing blackbush zone populations, when provided with *Atriplex* leaves in the post-weaning period, maintain weight when tested on an exclusive diet of *Atriplex* leaves.

This experiment was intended to test for the presence of developmental flexibility according to the model of Levins (1963). While at first glance it seems to show that the *Atriplex*-foraging mode can be elicited in young *D. microps* from blackbush habitats by exposure during a critical period of development, another possibility has not been eliminated by this demonstration. Namely, that the *Atriplex*-manipulating behavior is inherent to all members of the species and that it can be expressed in either young or adult individuals if given sufficient experience with this food item. Only by controlling the environment of individuals long enough to make certain the presumed critical period during which development is modifiable has passed, then attempting to switch them to the other ecological morph, can the theory of developmental flexibility be confirmed. This is difficult to do in the laboratory; however, if this sort of imprinting is the mechanism of adaptation operative in *D. microps,* then the experiment is already being performed in nature. The critical test, then, is to manipulate the environment of adults already past the hypothetical critical period of exposure. If they can be induced to display the resource-use patterns of the other ecological morph of the species, then the theory of permanent developmental adjustment can be rejected as a mechanism of adaptation in this species. This test is presented in Experiment V.

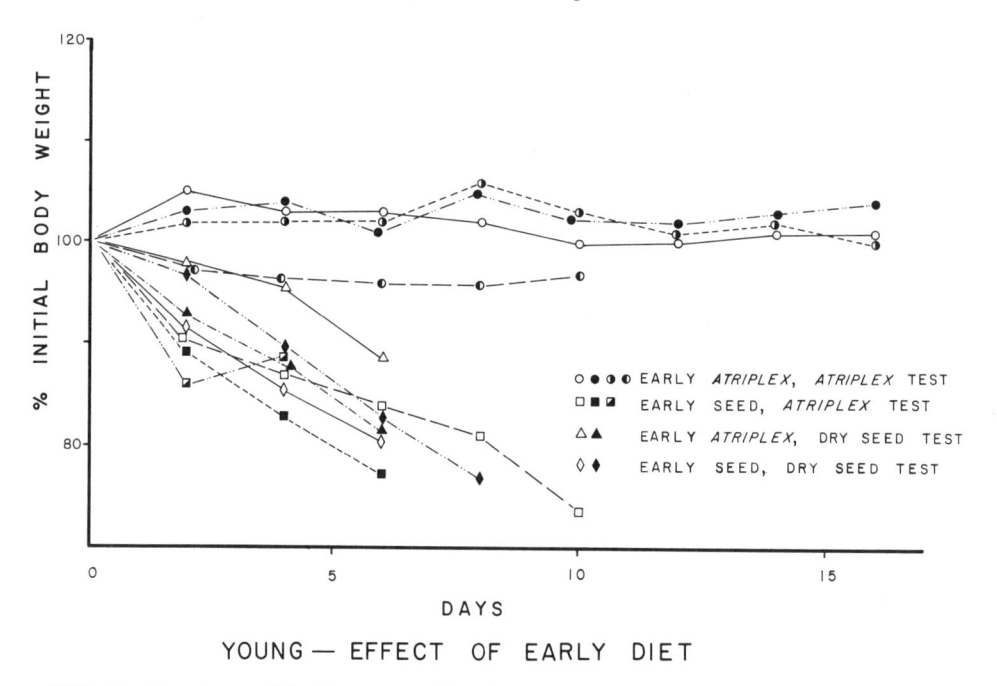

FIG. 11. Experiment III: Response of captive-born young *Dipodomys microps* to different dietary regimes. Symbols are used to indicate different early and late diets. Location of the source populations of the specimens used in this experiment are given in table 15. Each line represents the record of a single individual.

Experiment IV

Since not even blackbush zone adults successfully maintained weight on dry diets in the Bishop animal room, but had at Berkeley, I undertook rearing experiments with young in the animal room at Berkeley, where the higher relative humidity may be the critical factor allowing some *D. microps* to survive on a water-restricted regime. Since no source of *Atriplex confertifolia* is available near Berkeley, the tests performed during the spring and summer of 1975 had a narrower focus: to study the effect of water-restricted early diets on later water balance characteristics of *D. microps*.

Female *D. microps* suspected of being pregnant were returned to Berkeley after collecting trips to both study sites in early March and late April, 1975. During lactation, lettuce was provided nursing females *ad libitum*. Towards the end of this period, the young began to sample this food, so litters were separated from their mothers at 4-4½ weeks of age. Following weaning, each young animal was caged individually and given either seed and lettuce *ad libitum* or seed and minimal lettuce. Growth records were maintained and the minimal lettuce requirement was determined by maintaining slow but steady weight gain. Young fed lettuce *ad libitum* gained weight rapidly. These early experience diets were continued for four to six weeks. To more accurately simulate the slow drying of vegetation that would be experienced by field populations, a transition period of gradual removal of the lettuce supplement was initiated for both groups of young prior to testing the response of the animals to seed-only diets. This transition period lasted 17 or 18 days (2½ weeks). Animals were weighed during this period to insure that their condition did not deteriorate. All specimens were then placed on a dry seed diet to simulate conditions experienced in late summer or early fall in the blackbush environments.

I anticipated one of two possible outcomes from this experiment. If the ability to survive on restricted-water regimes has its basis in genetic adaptation, those young from Wolf Hole should perform better in seed-only feeding trials, regardless of treatment. If, however, acclimation takes place in early development and the range of physiological response in later life is altered by this early experience, then I would expect animals given large amounts of succulent lettuce in the post-weaning period to lose weight more rapidly than a similar group given minimal water when both were tested on seed-only diets, regardless of their parental locality.

No consistent trends were observed, nor was there any significant difference in performance between young of different early treatments or of different parental localities (fig. 12). None of the young tested were able to maintain weight on water-restricted diets. Some young from each treatment and some from each parental stock maintained weight both better than average and worse than average in these trials. Individual variation seemed to exceed any treatment or locality related patterns. Since field-caught adult samples do show a differential response to water deprivation experiments under some circumstances, these results suggest the laboratory environment is so artificial with respect to the environmental factors patterning development and/or acclimation of the species that experimental manipulation is difficult if not impossible. A repetition of Experiment I remains essential to demonstrate the species' potential to acclimate and thereby survive dry seasons in deciduous blackbush habitats. The gradual drying associated with the climate and phenology of this region will provide a natural transition from the leafy diet of springtime to the granivorous diet of fall (table 10).

YOUNG — EFFECT OF EARLY DIET, DRY SEED TEST DIET

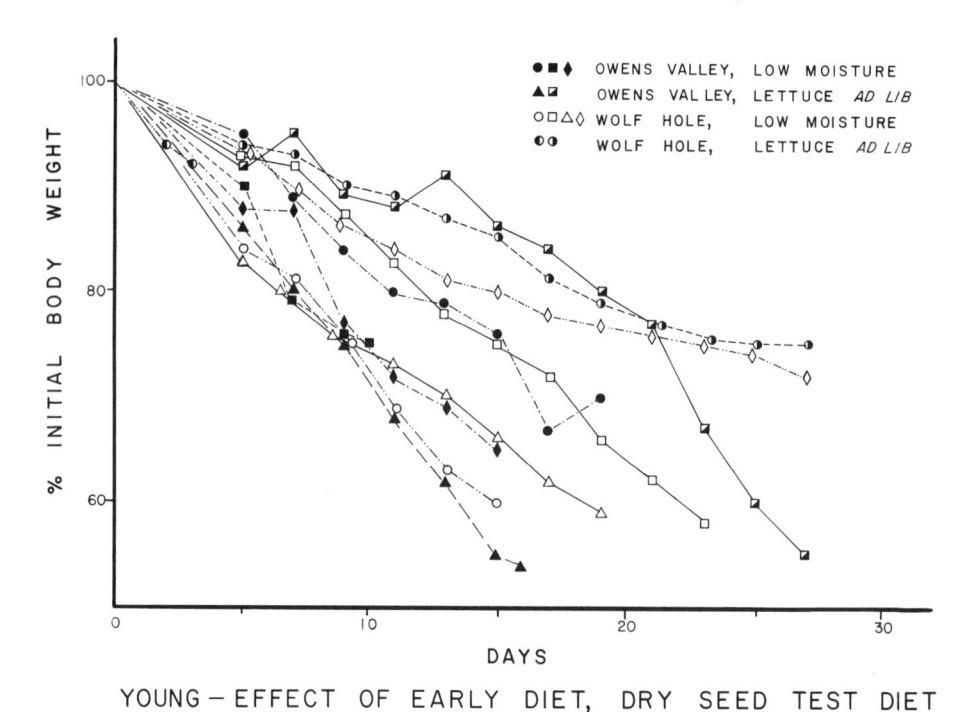

FIG. 12. Experiment IV: Weight maintenance of eleven captive-born young on dry seed diets at Berkeley following different early treatments. Symbols indicate locality of the source population and early treatment. Each line represents the record of a single individual.

Experiment V

Results of Experiment III indicated that at least some adults from the Wolf Hole population are able to adapt to a diet of *Atriplex* leaves and display the species-specific behavior pattern of leaf-shaving described by Kenagy (1973b). This plant is absent from the *Coleogyne* zone, where *Dipodomys microps* is granivorous. The previous failure of most specimens from these populations to use this food item suggests a need to further investigate the ability of these populations to engage in this specialized pattern of resource exploitation which would seem to be of little adaptive value in non-*Atriplex* habitats.

If the expression of one or another of the species' behavioral and physiological responses is determined non-genetically at an early age, then few if any Wolf Hole adults should successfully use *Atriplex* as a food item. If the observed differences in adaptive strategy between the two habitats is solely the result of genetic divergence accompanying ecological race formation, again, few if any Wolf Hole specimens should be able to express the *Atriplex*-shaving behavior pattern. If, on the other hand, the ability to use *Atriplex* is inherent to all populations of *D. microps* and most individuals are capable of expressing the leaf-eating adaptive strategy when given an adequate learning experience, then we may describe *Dipodomys microps* as a species having a "general purpose" genotype. The critical factor in determining the dimensions of the realized niche in this last case would be long periods of acclimation to habitats with different food resources. Given such a learning period, individuals could modify their behavior so as to conform to the strategy of populations native to that habitat.

Experiment V was designed to test for the presence of the *Atriplex*-foraging mode among *Dipodomys microps* populations native to the blackbush zone. Young born in the laboratory were tested on a specific aspect of early development: the effect of prior exposure to *Atriplex* leaves on the ability to use this food item in later life, regardless of area of origin.

During the spring of 1976, specimens of *D. microps* were collected from both *Atriplex* and *Coleogyne* habitats. Animals were transported to the White Mountain Research Station before weaning of the oldest young of the year to insure that exposure to test conditions could begin immediately after weaning. A smaller animal room (13½ x 14½ ft.) adjacent to the previously used facilities was modified to more nearly simulate conditions that would be encountered by free-living populations. An evaporative air cooler was installed in one wall and a screened opening to the outside was provided in an adjacent wall to allow exhaust of air from the room. This air circulation system maintained the temperature between 65° and 80°F (18-27°C) and the relative humidity between 44% and 58%. No artificial lighting was used, the open window providing photoperiods typical of 37° N latitude.

Specimens were captured on field trips between 23 March and 4 May, 1976. They were fed diets of wild bird seed and lettuce *ad libitum* between time of capture and transfer to Bishop on 18 May 1976. During this experiment all animals were housed individually in polyethylene cages which provided no opportunity for visual transferral of behavior patterns.

Owens Valley animals, native to *Atriplex* habitats, were divided into two groups. The first group (n=9) was immediately placed in cleaned cages and provided only with foliage of *Atriplex confertifolia* as a food item. Approximately 500 g of fresh *Atriplex* foliage was provided daily. The second group (n=7) was maintained in similar cages, except a supplement of seed was provided in addition to fresh *Atriplex* foliage for a period of 70 days, following which their cages were cleaned and only *Atriplex* was provided as a food item.

Wolf Hole animals were divided into three groups of 11 animals each. The first group was placed on a diet of *Atriplex* leaves immediately upon arrival in the Owens Valley. The second was given seed, lettuce, and fresh *Atriplex* leaves daily for 35 days, then placed on an *Atriplex*-only diet. The third group was maintained on seed and lettuce with fresh *Atriplex* foliage for 70 days, then transferred to *Atriplex*-only diets. All subgroups placed on *Atriplex* diets were maintained on that regime for 34 days. An individual was removed from the test if it lost more than 20% of initial body weight. Previous experiments indicated that after a loss of 20% of initial body weight the incidence of mortality rose sharply, and such loss was considered to be evidence of an inability to use *Atriplex* as a food item.

Captive-born young were divided into two test groups, each group containing individuals representing both parental localities. One group (n=6) was maintained on a diet of seed, lettuce, and breeding feed (described by Chew, 1958, for experiments with *D. merriami*) for a period of nine weeks. This group was then abruptly shifted to a diet of *Atriplex* leaves and maintained on this diet until individual weight losses exceeded 20% of initial body weight or until the end of the experiment. The second group (n=5) was given the same diet as the first during the initial post-weaning month with the addition of 500 g of fresh *Atriplex* foliage daily. Following one month of this regime, supplements of seed and lettuce were gradually reduced for a period of five weeks, until finally the group was shifted to an *Atriplex* leaf diet simultaneously with the first group.

Adults. Specimens from Wolf Hole showed marked improvement in ability to use *Atriplex* leaves as food with increasing opportunity for experimentation with these leaves (figs. 13-15). Differences were significant between animals with no prior exposure and animals given both five and ten weeks exposure, although the latter two did not differ at the $p=.05$ level. In terms of animals surviving to the end of the test period (n=11 for all trials), only three survived without prior exposure to *Atriplex* leaves; seven survived following five weeks exposure prior to testing; and all eleven survived following ten weeks opportunity to experiment with this food item.

WOLF HOLE ADULTS — IMMEDIATE *ATRIPLEX*

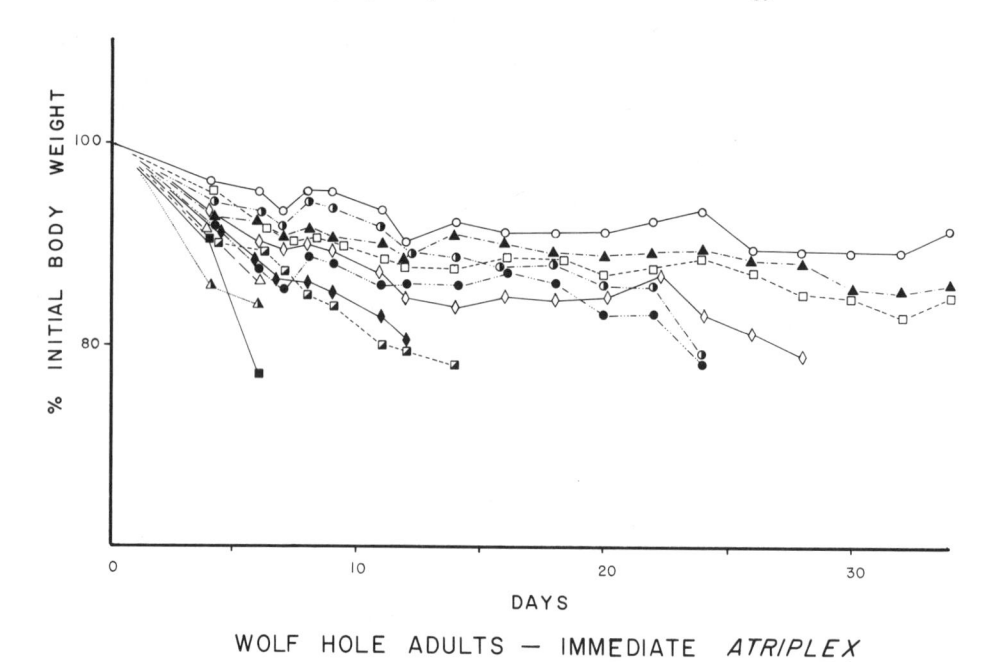

FIG. 13. Experiment V: Weight maintenance of 11 Wolf Hole adults on *Atriplex* leaf diets with no prior exposure to this food item. Average terminal weight of survivors (n=3) was 87% of original value. Each line represents the record of a single individual.

WOLF HOLE ADULTS — *ATRIPLEX*, 35 DAYS EXPOSURE

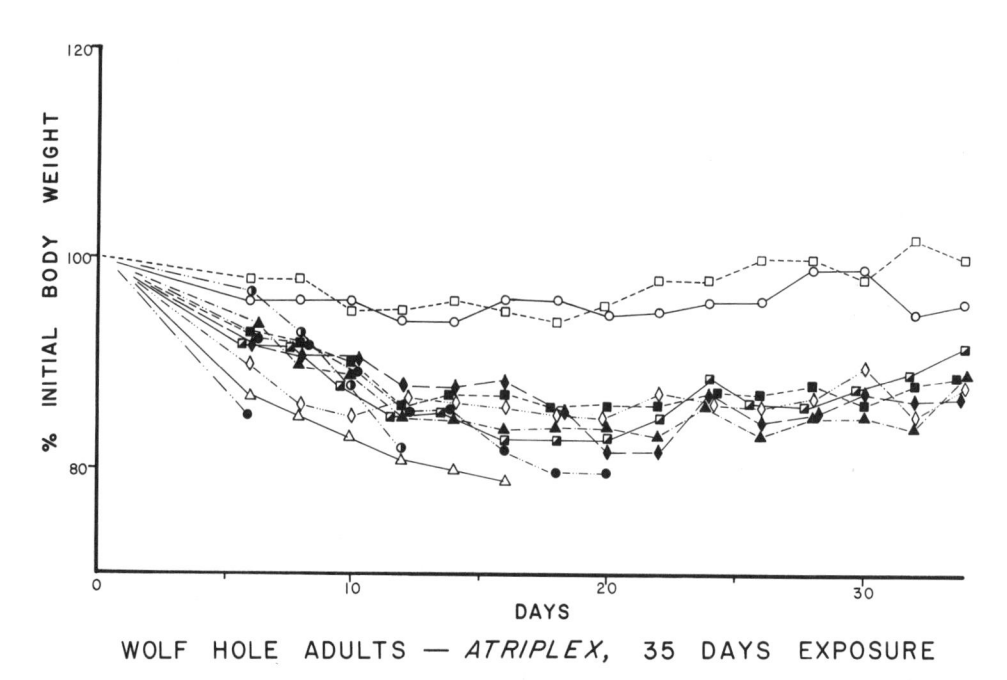

FIG. 14. Experiment V: Weight maintenance of 11 Wolf Hole adults on *Atriplex* leaf diets after 35 days exposure to this food item. Average terminal weight of survivors (n=7) was 92% of original value. Each line represents the record of a single individual.

WOLF HOLE ADULTS — *ATRIPLEX*, 70 DAYS EXPOSURE

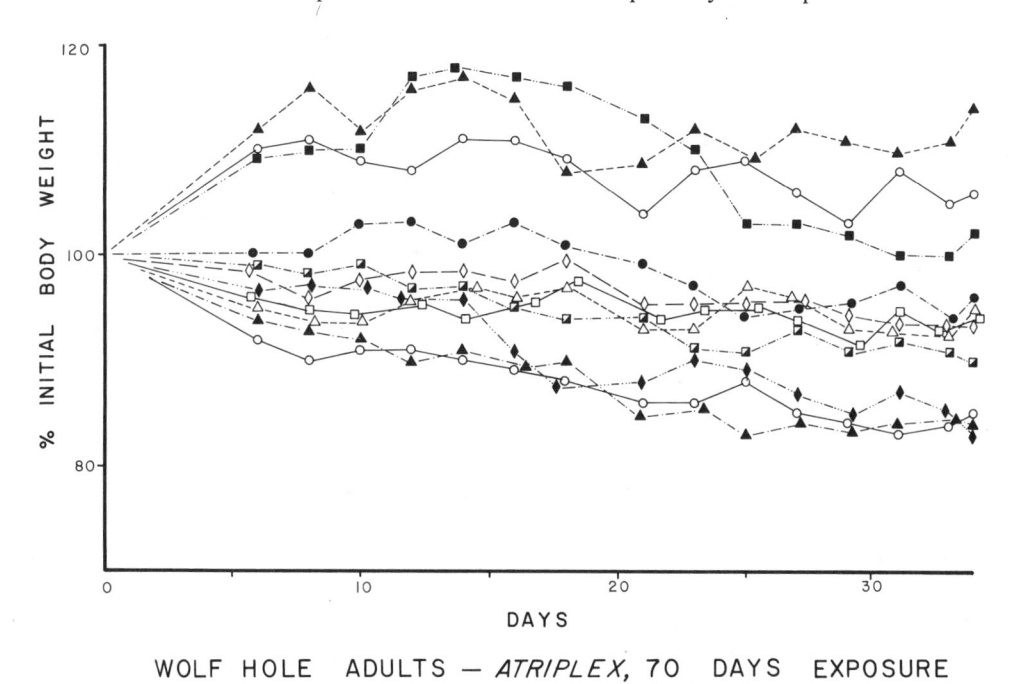

FIG. 15. Experiment V: Weight maintenance of 11 Wolf Hole adults on *Atriplex* leaf diets after 70 days exposure to this food item. Average terminal weight was 95% of initial value. All 11 individuals survived. Each line represents the record of a single individual.

OWENS VALLEY ADULTS — IMMEDIATE *ATRIPLEX*

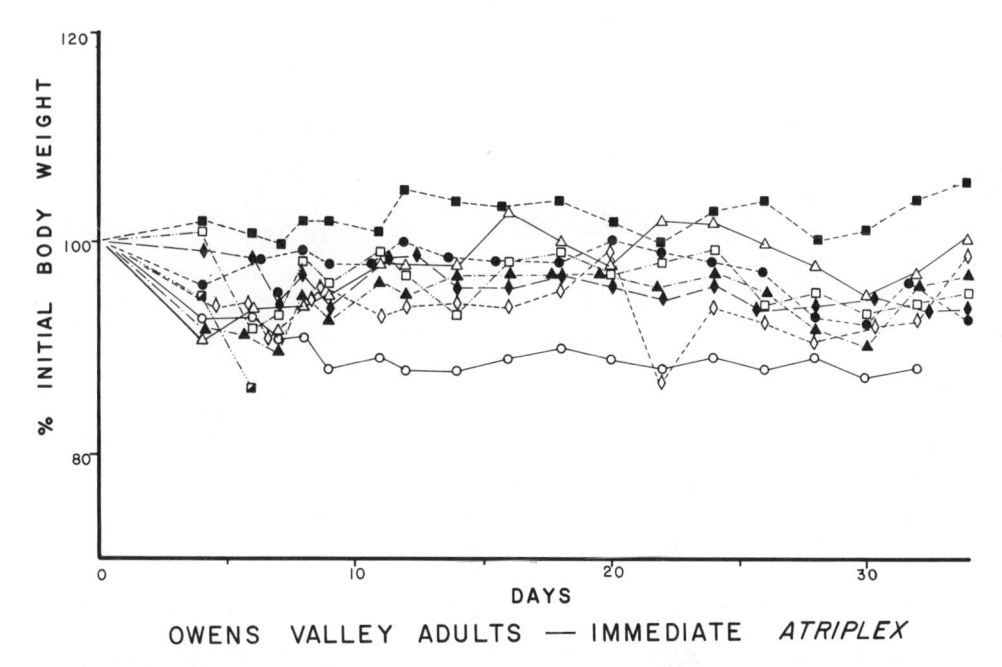

FIG. 16. Experiment V: Weight maintenance of nine Owens Valley adults on *Atriplex* leaf diets immediately following transfer to Bishop. Average terminal weight of survivors (n=7) was 98% of initial value. Each line represents the record of a single individual.

With two exceptions of unexplained mortality, all Owens Valley specimens survived to the end of the test period (figs. 16 and 17), although specimens given ten weeks seed-supplemented *Atriplex* prior to testing on an all-*Atriplex* diet did significantly better on that regime than those placed on an *Atriplex*-only diet immediately upon arrival from Berkeley. It is likely that the two- to three-month diet of seed and lettuce provided at Berkeley diminished the animal's behavioral and/or physiological capacity to secure nutrition from saltbush leaves.

If one compares the performance of sample populations from the two localities during simultaneous test runs, it is apparent that the Owens Valley group was significantly more efficient at using *Atriplex* as a food item, both initially and following ten weeks exposure to the leaves. Performance was improved in both samples when given increased time to experiment with *Atriplex* leaves. The test results from the Wolf Hole sample given ten weeks exposure to *Atriplex* do not differ significantly from those of the Owens Valley specimens placed on *Atriplex* immediately upon return from Berkeley.

Young. Data for these specimens are summarized in table 16. Difficulties in interpretation were encountered due to the small size of the subgroups (n=1, 2, 3). Statistical analysis was not attempted for these results. No consistent differences were noted in the ability to maintain weight on *Atriplex* leaves between young of different source populations or between young given different post-weaning treatments. Any inherent ability to use *Atriplex* leaves more efficiently present in the Owens Valley population was not displayed by these young. Further, young from the *Coleogyne* locality that were given early exposure to *Atriplex* maintained weight more successfully than those from the *Atriplex* locality denied experience with the food item. These comparisons suggest that experience with a food item is critical and that

OWENS VALLEY ADULTS — *ATRIPLEX*, 70 DAYS EXPOSURE

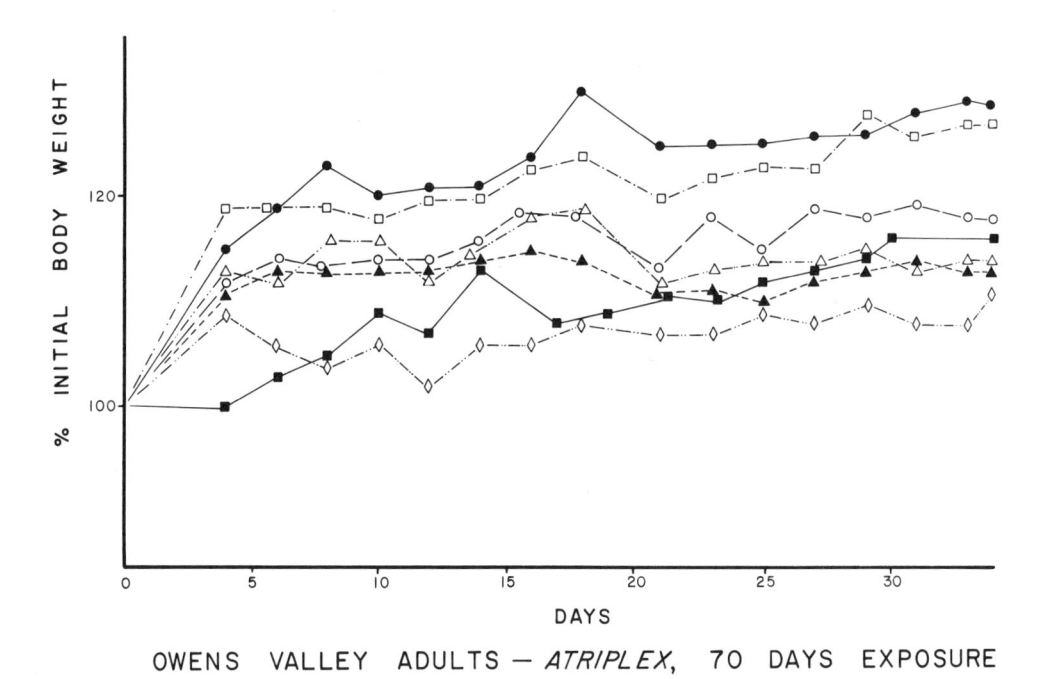

FIG. 17. Experiment V: Weight maintenance of seven Owens Valley adults on *Atriplex* leaf diets following 70 days supplemented exposure to this food item. Average terminal weight was 112% of initial value. All seven specimens survived. Each line represents the record of a single individual.

TABLE 16. EXPERIMENT V. EXPERIMENTAL DESIGN AND RESULTS OF FEEDING TRIALS WITH CAPTIVE-BORN YOUNG
(Test duration, 34 days)

Locality of parental population	Early diet	Test diet	Specimen number	Days survived	Percent original weight at termination
Owens Valley	Atriplex, seed, lettuce	Atriplex	194a*	34	103
	Atriplex, seed, lettuce	Atriplex	254b	30	85
	seed, lettuce	Atriplex	194b	34	84
	seed, lettuce	Atriplex	194c	34	86
	seed, lettuce	Atriplex	254a	3	85
Wolf Hole	Atriplex, seed, lettuce	Atriplex	190a	34	95
	Atriplex, seed, lettuce	Atriplex	192a	34	97
	Atriplex, seed, lettuce	Atriplex	193a	34	99
	seed, lettuce	Atriplex	191b	10	81
	seed, lettuce	Atriplex	192b	30	95
	seed, lettuce	Atriplex	193b	34	100
Owens Valley (control)	seed, lettuce	seed, lettuce	274a	34	106

*Lower case letters following specimen numbers are used to identify offspring (e.g., 254a and 254b are captive-born offspring of specimen No. 254, captured in the Owens Valley).

this environmental factor overrides genetic differences between the populations. Moreover, the only young which lost weight rapidly were two of the six without exposure to *Atriplex* during their post-weaning period (191b, 254b).

Taking the results with both adults and young into account, I conclude that exposure to *Atriplex* is of considerable, perhaps overriding, importance in determining subsequent performance with this food item. These experiments suggest that *D. microps* has the potential to follow a generalist strategy, whereby each population may follow an exploitation system adjusted to the local resource base.

Experiment VI

On 26 September 1976, I collected a series of 15 adult *D. microps* at Wolf Hole to conduct a water deprivation experiment at Berkeley. A sample of animals born in the spring of 1976 whose feeding history consisted of an uninterrupted supply of succulent food (either lettuce or *Atriplex* leaves) was tested simultaneously on the same water-restricted regime. Animals were housed individually in polyethylene cages and given wild bird mix in excess. As little lettuce as possible was provided during transport of specimens from Wolf Hole to Berkeley, although some was given to avoid desiccation and loss of condition during the trip back through the Mojave Desert. The test was initiated immediately upon their return.

Eleven of fifteen adults completed the experiment, the average weight of survivors being 104% of their original weight (fig. 18). Seven of the original 15 animals gained weight on a dry seed diet during the course of the experiment, while eight lost weight. A comparison of these results with those reported for Experiment I reveals no significant differences ($p=.05$).

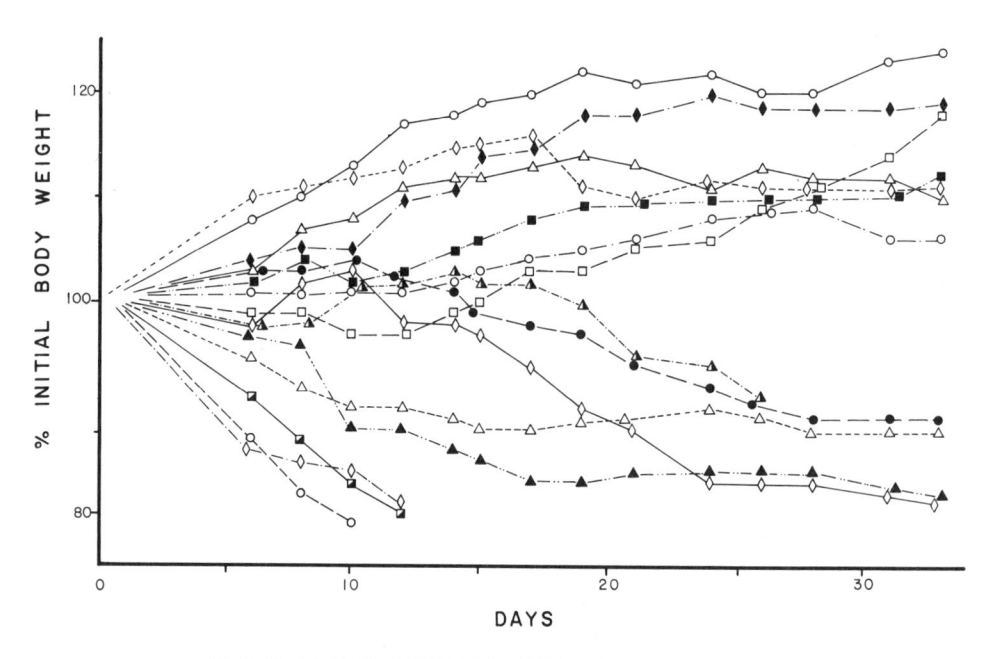

WOLF HOLE ADULTS, DRY SEED DIET (BERKELEY)

FIG. 18. Experiment VI: Weight maintenance of 15 fall-caught Wolf Hole adults on dry seed diets at Berkeley. Average terminal weight of survivors (n=11) was 104% of initial weight. Each line represents the record of a single individual.

Despite the presence of considerable individual variation (fig. 18), this experiment demonstrates that *D. microps* populations from blackbush habitats have the capacity to physiologically acclimate to conditions of water deprivation. This concurs with the suggestion that the occupancy of habitats dominated by deciduous shrubs depends on exploitation of an abundant seed resource and survival of the drier months by behavioral and physiological adjustments, even though considerable moisture may be required during the spring for successful breeding. A generalized *heermanni* group foraging strategy is available to *D. microps* in the *Coleogyne* zone, as well as the *Atriplex*-browsing strategy described for saltbush zone populations. At least for members of the Wolf Hole population, a transition between these strategies is possible through the mechanism of acclimation.

None of the lab-reared specimens survived the term of the experiment, all losing at least 20% of their initial body weight (table 17). These results differ significantly from those of field-caught fall-adults from Wolf Hole, and further confirm the suggestion that prior exposure to xeric conditions is required to enable the species to maintain weight on a dry seed diet. Ironically, young of Owens Valley parentage survived longer in this test than those of Wolf Hole parentage. Initial body weights of the Wolf Hole specimens were higher and therefore the absolute rate of weight loss was greater in this subgroup. There was no correlation among the young between superior weight maintenance and the previous type of succulent vegetation provided. All young received similar treatment during the two months preceding the experiment. In view of their similar histories, this result suggests genetic differentiation between populations of *D. microps*, but suggests unexpectedly that the Owens Valley population is better able to cope with moisture stress under laboratory conditions. Laboratory rearing does not expose young to stresses comparable to the field situation. Although differ-

TABLE 17. EXPERIMENT VI. WEIGHT MAINTENANCE AND SURVIVAL OF LAB-REARED *DIPODOMYS MICROPS* ON DRY SEED DIETS AT U. C. BERKELEY
(Test duration, 33 days)

Specimen number	Initial body weight (g)	Days survived	Percent original weight
Owens Valley			
194a	54	19	75
194b	61	31	80
194c	62	12	77
254a	64	10	77
254b	55	15	78
247a	68	21	78
	$\bar{x} = 60$		$\bar{x} = 78$
Wolf Hole			
192a	69	6	75
192b	62	5	77
193a	77	6	79
193b	69	3	81
	$\bar{x} = 69$		$\bar{x} = 79$

Wilcoxon Two-Sample test for difference in survival and terminal weight between localities: significant at $p \geqslant .01$.

ences observed between young from the two localities may relate to totally different field parameters, they may also preadapt one or the other group to certain laboratory conditions. Further studies are planned to investigate the development of water balance mechanisms in these two populations.

Summary of Feeding Experiments

The foregoing experiments were undertaken to assess the role of inherent and non-genetic components of variation in food niche and foraging strategy in populations of *D. microps* from different habitats. Initially three mechanisms were proposed to account for the observed variation in habitat use. These were: (1) ecotypic differentiation may have occurred, so that populations have distinct genetically-controlled adaptations; (2) the species may be an operational generalist, most individuals having the ability to shift their realized niche by virtue of a broad behavioral and physiological capacity for response to different resource bases; and (3) response to the early environment, through the mechanism of developmental flexibility, results in one or another adaptive expression of the genotype being carried over to the adult phenotype.

Early experiments (I and II) demonstrated basic behavioral and physiological differences between two populations, which may have been the result of selection for different adaptive modes. Experiment III generally agreed with earlier experiments, but provided the first hint that adult Wolf Hole animals may display behavior patterns appropriate to the *Atriplex*-browsing strategy. Captive-born young raised at this time clearly indicated the browsing pattern is contained within the genetic make-up of the blackbush populations and was inducible, perhaps by changes in developmental pathways or by acclimation.

Attempts to induce xeric adaptations in young similar to those seen in *Coleogyne* zone adults were unsuccessful in Experiment IV, and there were no consistent differences between young from either locality. During Experiment V young were again given variable exposure to *Atriplex* leaves during development. Although individual variation obscured results, the trends of Experiment III were repeated and early experience tended to result in more efficient handling of this food item. Simultaneously, it was demonstrated that adult animals from both localities could respond to *Atriplex* leaves with the correct species-specific behavior pattern, and that efficiency improved (especially among blackbush zone adults) with greater opportunity to experiment with this novel food item. No irreversible changes seem to occur during development of this species which preclude granivorous adult specimens from shifting their pattern of resource use to phytophagy. This shift involves development of previously dormant complex behavior patterns associated with leaf-shaving, not merely adjusting to a new food type. I therefore conclude that the ecological polymorphism in *D. microps* is not achieved through the mechanism of developmental flexibility, but at least partly through possession of a general purpose genotype. Finally, Experiment VI again confirmed that a majority of fall-caught blackbush zone adults can survive extended periods without access to succulent vegetation, some gaining weight in the process. Simultaneous tests with sub-adults known to have had water-enriched feeding histories provided a striking contrast, these animals rapidly losing weight under the same conditions.

Evidence seems to favor the hypothesis that *D. microps* is primarily a generalist, and that members of any population can be induced to shift their food niche and associated physiology and behavior when placed in a condition simulating other habitats occupied by the species, as long as the shift is not too abrupt. A genetic component is also present in this adaptation, however, for Owens Valley animals not only are consistently more efficient at *Atriplex* browsing, but they do not seem as competent at coping with moisture stress as Wolf Hole specimens.

DISCUSSION

MECHANISMS OF ADAPTATION IN *DIPODOMYS MICROPS*

The system of adaptation observed in *D. microps* seems to contain elements of both ecotypic differentiation and phenotypic plasticity. Differences in cranial morphology and pelage color have long formed the basis of subspecific recognition, and they presumably indicate a degree of genetic differentiation among populations of the species. Although the morphology of the lower incisors, a diagnostic character for the species, did not vary among populations whose actual use of the incisors varies, it was shown that populations from non-*Atriplex* environments could use their chisel-shaped lower incisors efficiently to shave *Atriplex* leaves under appropriate circumstances. Differences in bacular morphology and kidney weight help confirm the presence of underlying genetic differentiation in the species. Electrophoretic evidence allowed the assessment of the relative magnitude of intraspecific genetic divergence, which was correlated with geographic distance between populations rather than with any habitat-related factor.

It is obvious that nearly all species show components of both genetic and physiological variation. One may therefore expect to find both mechanisms of adaptation at work in a population at any one time. Through physiological response a species may exploit a variety of habitats, but given sufficient time and appropriate selection pressure, genetic differences will develop between populations.

Within *D. microps* I observed a considerable amount of individual variation in the responses to various experimental conditions (e.g., fig. 18). This variation would seem to indicate a lack of fixation of any particular set of characters in the genotype of either population. There is still much genetic similarity between populations of *Dipodomys microps,* and a generalized genotype, responsive to selection pressures towards *Atriplex*-browsing or towards granivory, seems common to many populations. Although the ability to shave saltbush leaves is genetically coded in all the populations I studied and is, perhaps, maintained by limited gene flow with nearby *Atriplex*-feeding populations, those populations that have been resident in *Atriplex* habitat the longest (e.g., northern-central Nevada, the Owens Valley) are beginning to show the results of selection for the *Atriplex*-browsing genotype. Owens Valley adults were consistently more efficient at using *Atriplex* leaves than even the best "educated" Wolf Hole specimens (Experiment V).

The species seems to represent an intermediate stage in the formation of ecological races. In the southwestern portion of the range, populations with different karyotypes (Yucca Valley and Joshua Tree) occupy the same habitat and presumably share their realized niches. On biochemical grounds, they are more closely related to the nearby *Atriplex*-browsing populations in the Antelope and Owens Valleys than they are to the Wolf Hole population to the east, whose habitat and granivorous strategy they share. The ecological demands of the habitat determine which portion of the species' niche will be realized. These environmental factors override the genetic similarity between the Joshua Tree and Antelope-Owens Valley populations or the genetic distance between Joshua Tree and Wolf Hole populations. The wide range of physiological response within the species allows populations to exploit a variety of habitats that would be impossible were populations already ecotypically differentiated specialists.

I hypothesized that my inability to repeat the results of Experiment I, in which Wolf Hole adults maintained weight on dry seed diets, was due in part to low atmospheric moisture content in the Bishop animal room and in part to seasonal variation in the physiological capabilities of animals from this locality due to a gradual shift in their diet towards granivory in the fall of the year. The vapor pressure of water in the atmosphere more accurately reflects the role of pulmocutaneous water loss from an animal than the relative humidity. Since my experiments were carried out in rooms of approximately equal temperature, relative humidity is correlated with vapor pressure. Table 18 summarizes the temperature and humidity of the animal room environment for each experiment. Since both temperature and humidity varied within a certain range, comparisons were made using values I considered modal for each situation. Some specimens were maintained on dry seed diets in all but Experiment V, although the field and laboratory history of these specimens varied between experiments. Similar atmospheric humidities prevailed during Experiments I and VI, where fall-caught Wolf Hole adults maintained weight on dry seed diets. The lowest vapor pressures were encountered in Experiment II, during which fall-caught specimens that had previously maintained weight on dry diets could not repeat this performance at Bishop. Both Experiments III and IV were conducted under somewhat higher humidity levels than Experiment II, but animals fed dry diets during these tests may not have been acclimated to minimal water regimes by either

TABLE 18. HUMIDITY OF ANIMAL ROOMS USED IN LABORATORY EXPERIMENTS
(vapor pressure in millimeters of mercury)*

Experiment number	Location	Date	Temperature-range, mode	% relative humidity-range, mode	Vapor pressure (in mm Hg)
I	Berkeley	Aug-Sep 1973	70-80°F 75°F	50-60% 50%	10.97
II	Bishop	Nov 1973	68-80°F 75°F	10-20% 20%	4.37
III	Bishop	Jun-Jul 1974	72-83°F 77°F	23-38% 30%	7.06
IV	Berkeley	May-Aug 1975	61-75°F 69°F	50-60% 50%	8.81
V	Bishop	Jun-Sep 1976	68-82°F 75°F	44-72% 55%	12.24
VI	Berkeley	Oct 1976	65-72°F 68°F	50-60% 50%	8.81

*Absolute humidities are computed from relative humidity and air temperature, using tables by Marvin, 1941.

field or laboratory experiences. It appears that the ability to survive on dry diets is correlated with both ambient vapor pressure and physiological state in *D. microps*.

Although no data are available for the burrow environments of *D. microps* in the two study areas, some predictions can be made based on other data. Weather records indicate both higher summer temperatures and rainfall at Wolf Hole. Beatley (1976b) attributes the limitation of *D. microps* to the *Coleogyne* zones in southern Nevada to higher ground moisture and consequently higher burrow humidity than would be present in the creosote bush community. If burrow temperatures are higher at Wolf Hole, then the water vapor pressure in the burrow environment would be much higher in this habitat, enhancing the ability of a water-stressed population of *D. microps* to survive periods when succulent vegetation is unavailable. In the southern Great Basin granivorous populations of the species are found in the moister blackbush zone, whereas the species occurs in the relatively arid *Atriplex* zone both in the Owens Valley and at lower elevations in southern Utah (Hardy, 1945). As at my Owens Valley site, the species presumably escapes moisture stress in this community by its succulent diet. Two different strategies of adaptation to arid environments are thus present in the same species of desert rodent.

The results of my laboratory experiments support the hypothesis that humidity is a critical factor for survival of *D. microps* in the *Coleogyne* zone. Mullen (1971) also reports a high rate of water turnover in *D. microps* from southern Nevada, as compared to *D. merriami* from the same region. The need for water conservation in *D. microps* would seem to parallel the situation reported for *D. agilis* by Carpenter (1966), *D. venustus* by Church (1969), and *D. panamintinus* by Nichter (1957). While not independent of succulent vegetation, stress is minimized by behavioral mechanisms during the driest parts of the year, when the diet consists primarily of dry seeds. Moisture absorbed by food in burrow caches has been suggested as a further mechanism for water conservation in the genus, and again the higher soil moisture in the *Coleogyne* zone would increase the importance of this source of water. Kenagy (1973a) suggests that the heteromyid rodents he studied in the Owens Valley engaged in daily subterranean movements as a mechanism of behavioral thermoregulation. Such movements may also be influenced by burrow vapor pressure gradients during periods of water stress.

The greater size of the kidneys from Owens Valley specimens of *D. microps*, both relatively and absolutely, indicates this population may be adapted to function under greater osmotic stress than the Wolf Hole population. Differences in renal anatomy and physiology may be correlated with several types of osmotic stress. In the absence of both water and succulent vegetation, *D. merriami* produces a small volume of highly concentrated urine (Schmidt-Nielsen and Schmidt-Nielsen, 1952). Schmidt-Nielsen and O'Dell (1961) and Schmidt-Nielsen, B., (1964) present data on the kidney of *Psammomys obesus*, which is specialized for excreting a large volume of highly concentrated urine. In contrast to a granivore with a restricted water intake, such as *D. merriami*, *Psammomys* feeds on succulent chenopods such as *Traganum* and *Salicornia* (Harrison, D. L., 1972), which are up to 82.6% water but have a high salt concentration. *Psammomys obesus* must excrete a large volume of concentrated urine to dissipate the salt load acquired while feeding. A species such as *D. merriami* is adapted to a granivorous diet and can survive without access to succulent vegetation of any sort. While such a species concentrates its urine as much as *Psammomys*, the volume is necessarily much less. All loops of Henle are long in the *Psammomys* kidney, whereas only 25% are long loops in *D. merriami*, reflecting the increased urinary capacity of the former species (Schmidt-Nielsen, B., 1964).

The difference observed between kidney sizes of the two *D. microps* populations I examined may well represent an analogous situation correlated with different selective pressures arising from dietary dissimilarities. Since the *Atriplex* zone populations feed primarily on leaves high in both salt and water content, and the *Coleogyne* zone populations are more or less granivorous, often surviving the summer and fall without access to succulents, the greater absolute and relative kidney size of the Owens Valley specimens may indicate greater osmotic stresses and the need to excrete a larger quantity of concentrated urine. Adaptation to a dry seed diet, however, would require production of a small amount of urine with a high urea concentration. Schmidt-Nielsen and O'Dell (1961) note that *P. obesus* is unable to concentrate urea as well as *D. merriami*. It may well be that two different kidney functions are being selected for in *D. microps:* (1) large urine volume with high electrolyte concentration; and (2) small volumes of urine with high urea concentrations. The observed differences in kidney size support this hypothesis.

Similar complex patterns of adaptation have created difficulties in other studies dealing with physiological ecology below the species level. For example, Cade and Bartholomew (1959) reported subspecific differences in tolerance to water deprivation in the Savannah Sparrow (*Passerculus sandwichensis*). Only the race *P. s. rostratus* was able to maintain weight while drinking sea water or when given a dry seed diet. This subspecies was represented by a single individual. Johnson and Ohmart (1973) attempted to duplicate these results with a larger series of specimens without success. They note the relative humidity in their experimental room was only 30% whereas that of Cade and Bartholomew (1959) was 40-70%, but they consider this factor unlikely to account for the difference in results.

The Savannah Sparrow, like *D. microps,* is a species with a number of ecological races displaying varying degrees of adaptation to water stress. In my attempts to measure resistance to water stress in Wolf Hole adults, I experienced similar difficulties in replicating my original results. Several factors seem to have interacted to create these difficulties: (1) in a dynamic system of ecotypic differentiation there is considerable variability in response within a population, individuals at the extremes of this response spectrum showing markedly different physiological capacities (Johnson and Ohmart illustrated a similar effect in their specimens of *P. s. rostratus* given 0.6 molar NaCl, three dying and three regaining weight after an initial loss and thereafter remaining stable); (2) in populations still in the process of adapting to xeric conditions, factors such as relative humidity seem very critical. The 25% difference in relative humidity between the two studies could have played a significant role in weight maintenance of experimental specimens; and (3) seasonal variation may occur in ability to resist water stress. The gradual drying of the natural environment results in acclimation which is difficult to simulate in the laboratory. No information is available on the seasonal status of the sparrows used in these two experiments.

I am inclined to believe that Cade and Bartholomew's (1959) results reflect an extreme physiological response in *P. s. rostratus* under optimum circumstances. The difficulties encountered duplicating results from experiments dealing with physiological races of vertebrate species in the present study and by Johnson and Ohmart (1973) help explain why genecology has been pursued more diligently by botanists.

PALAEOECOLOGY OF *DIPODOMYS MICROPS*

The ubiquity of granivory among heteromyids forces one to the conclusion that this was the adaptive strategy of the ancestral stock leading to *D. microps*. As Mayr (1963:573) points out, most species are made up of many populations, each adapted to a particular set of environmental conditions and usually with some restrictions to gene flow among them. For a population to invade a new niche, it must have a considerable range of tolerance to environmental conditions. If adaptations to the requirements of the new niche initially expand the set of adaptive responses possible in that population, then an ecological polymorphism will exist for a period of time. This process has been termed *annidation* by Ludwig (1950). In time, one would expect the new set of adaptations to replace a portion of the old, possibly accompanied by reproductive isolation of its carriers. Circumstances suggest such a process is operative in *D. microps*.

Lackey (1967b) summarizes the ecologic affinities of *heermanni* group species. The narrow-faced *agilis* subgroup tends to occupy chaparral covered slopes, whereas the broad-faced *heermanni* subgroup occurs in open habitat. The narrow-faced *D. peninsularis* shows habitat affinities tending towards those of the *heermanni* subgroup, indicating a common ancestral habitat of scattered shrubs. Evidence suggests an early divergence of *D. microps* from the *agilis-heermanni* lineage (Johnson and Selander, 1971; Stock, 1974). If adaptation to *Atriplex* foraging is the innovation which facilitated the occupancy of the central Great Basin by *D. microps*, then, prior to this adaptive shift, the ancestral populations could be hypothesized to have occupied areas not unlike those mountain slopes on which southern populations are found today. In the absence of *Atriplex confertifolia* as a resource, the adaptive strategy followed by the species in such areas closely resembles that of its *heermanni* group relatives.

Since *Atriplex* is evergreen, its leaves represent a continually available resource to species able to tolerate their high salt content. Sampson and Jespersen (1963) report the protein content of the leaves to be 5.6-8.9%. I determined the caloric equivalent of dry *Atriplex* leaves to be 3000 calories per gram by bomb calorimetry. This value compares favorably with figures for millet or wheat seed (3270 and 3000 cal/g, 11% water content, USDA, 1963). The high food value of *Atriplex* leaves renders them prime candidates for exploitation by a species preadapted to such a diet. It is probable that the initial use of vegetation in the developing Mojave Desert by *D. microps* (assuming the ancestral populations of the species entered the developing desert from the western metropolis of the *heermanni* group) was for its moisture content. Extant populations consume some *Atriplex* leaves without shaving during periods when leaf-water content is high. If nutritional requirements could be met simultaneously with water requirements, selection would favor specialization for use of such a superabundant resource.

It is extremely unlikely that *D. microps* acquired its diagnostic tooth morphology and adaptive strategy since the end of the Wisconsin glacial period, coincident with the drying of the Pleistocene lakes and formation of modern saltbush flats. Lidicker (1960a) placed the differentiation of modern *Dipodomys* species after the upper Pliocene. Similarly, Stock (1974) hypothesized that *D. microps* diverged from *heermanni* group ancestors during or since the middle Pleistocene. During the course of my biochemical investigations, I examined acrylamide gels of plasma proteins and liver esterases to estimate the genetic distance between *D. microps* and its *heermanni* group relatives (*D. agilis, D. heermanni, D. panamintinus*). Nei distances of 0.9 to 1.4 were calculated between *D. microps* and these related species. These results are of interest here because Nei distances derived from these rapidly evolving loci have been used to estimate divergence times of the lineages involved by Sarich (1977). At present, a Nei distance of 1.0 appears to represent separation of the taxa involved by about two to three million years. While this represents only a first approximation of the divergence time of these lineages (see Sarich, 1977, for details of this method), it is interesting that this date coincides with the appearance of modern desert vegetation (Axelrod, 1950) and with estimates of the age of *Dipodomys* species proposed by Lidicker (1960a) and Stock (1974).

Based on this information, I conclude that the geographic and ecologic divergence of *D. microps* from other *heermanni* group species most likely occurred in early Pleistocene times, coincident with the formation of the Great Basin Desert vegetation. Since Lackey (1967b) proposed the broad- and narrow-faced subgroups diverged in response to life in different habitats, the vegetational changes at the end of the Pliocene further support separation of the *agilis* and *heermanni* lineages during this period. It seems likely that, along with the formation of desert vegetation, this time period marks the beginning of the process of adaptation to *Atriplex*-browsing in *D. microps.*

BIOGEOGRAPHY OF *DIPODOMYS MICROPS*

Most animal species display a certain habitat specificity. The modern distribution of *D. microps* is roughly congruent with that of either *Atriplex confertifolia* or *Coleogyne ramosissima.* Evidence has accumulated during the last decade (Martin and Mehringer, 1965; Wells and Burger, 1967; Mehringer, 1967, 1977; King, 1976) documenting an elevational lowering of the current vegetational zones in the Mojave and Great Basin Deserts in response to cooler, moister climate during the late Pleistocene. The Wisconsin glacial period (ca. 70,000-10,000 B.P.) was accompanied by enlargement of the lakes of the Great Basin and a downward shift of the altitudinal range of plants by a minimum of 300-400 m (Mehringer, 1977). Martin and Mehringer (1965) present a map of the proposed full-glacial vegetation in the southwest. Evidence is strong to suggest that many areas currently in the Lower Sonoran zone (e.g., the Las Vegas Valley) were formerly (12,000-10,000 B.P.) juniper-sagebrush communities (Mehringer, 1967), whereas much of the modern *Coleogyne* zone was piñon-juniper woodland.

It may be presumed that there was an ebb and flow of Lower and Upper Sonoran animal species coincident with the changes in vegetation described above. The geographic location of habitat suitable for occupancy by *D. microps* must have undergone considerable altitudinal and some latitudinal migration during the Wisconsin period. Only within the last 10,000 years have desert vegetational zones assumed their modern limits. Since much of the present range of the species was unsuitable habitat until recent times (e.g., slopes of desert mountain ranges such as the 4750 ft. site of the Joshua Tree population), I conclude that current populations represent an expansion of the species from refugia occupied during the full Wisconsin glacial, some 20,000 years ago. Such a hypothesis agrees with Stock's (1974) suggestions based on karyological evidence, and would help explain the clinal nature of genetic divergence among *D. microps* populations in the Great Basin.

While the species currently possesses an adaptation for *Atriplex*-browsing which appears to be responsible for its success in the Great Basin Desert, the temporally unstable environments of the Pleistocene would have favored retention of unspecialized aspects of an ancestral adaptive strategy reminiscent of that of *heermanni* group relatives. The gene flow associated with isolation and subsequent reconnection of relictual populations would have prevented fixation of any specialized traits in the species' genome to the exclusion of general adaptability. The same process would enable all populations to acquire the genetic capability to exploit *Atriplex confertifolia* as a food source. Following the glacial retreat, some populations invaded the southern mountains with advancing *Coleogyne,* while others expanded northward through the central Great Basin with the expansion of *Atriplex confertifolia* into former lake basins. Modern populations now appear to be diverging in response to differential selection pressures in blackbush and saltbush habitats.

Aside from occupying the blackbush zone of southern Nevada and northwestern Arizona,

D. microps has been found in this vegetational association on isolated mountain slopes of southern California (Miller and Stebbins, 1964; present study). These populations are currently separated from neighboring populations of *D. m. occidentalis* by approximately 160 km of unsuitable Lower Sonoran habitat. Mehringer (1967:190) presents a map of the minimal extent of Pleistocene woodlands in the Mojave Desert during the period 22,000-12,500 B.P., indicating the piñon-juniper zone of the Providence Mountains area was separated from that of the San Bernardino Mountains by no more than 13 km (8 miles). Since the blackbush zone is found just below and grading into the piñon-juniper zone, it can be assumed that a continuous or nearly continuous connection of the *Coleogyne* association existed between the Kingston Range and Clark Mountain to the north and the San Bernardino and Little San Bernardino Mountains to the south during the late Pleistocene. Such an avenue of dispersal would help explain the presence of many transitional and boreal species in the isolated mountain ranges of the southern California desert today, in addition to providing a dispersal corridor through which *Dipodomys microps* could reach its modern southern limits.

In summary, I propose that *D. microps* entered the Great Basin from the west in the late Pliocene, coincident with adaptation to *Atriplex*-browsing. The Pleistocene glaciations isolated the species and spatially reduced its range. This temporal and spatial heterogeneity facilitated gene flow and favored retention of both seed and *Atriplex* feeding strategies. The post-glacial period saw an expansion of the species' range into both *Coleogyne* and lake-bed habitats, with incipient ecological race formation.

IMPLICATIONS OF GEOGRAPHIC VARIATION IN THE NICHE

It is quite possible that the differences in resource use patterns described for various populations of *D. microps* may in turn result in differences in life history strategies. Beatley (1969) and Bradley and Mauer (1971) present data indicating that the timing of reproduction in *D. microps* and *D. merriami* is in part dependent on availability of winter annuals. Kenagy (1973b) proposed that the former species may be independent of this source of water in the Owens Valley due to its ability to obtain moisture from the succulent but saline leaves of *Atriplex confertifolia*. The use of evergreen shrubs may allow successful breeding in the species independent of the growth of winter annuals. If, however, *D. microps* is following a strategy similar to that of *D. merriami* in the non-*Atriplex* parts of its range, then it may experience differential selection pressures influencing such factors as the timing of reproduction, litter size, and reproductive life span in different parts of its range. In short, changing the resource base of a species by either genetic or physiological mechanisms (or both, as in this instance) may have profound effects on many components of the fundamental niche.

Theoretical ecologists have proposed models by which species faced with environmental variation may respond through simple polymorphic systems (Levins, 1963, 1968). Although such models may be heuristically useful, it should be borne in mind that the components of an adaptive strategy are likely to be under the control of a constellation of individual genes. While linkage-groups may be formed to preserve well-adapted combinations of genes, or a single gene may direct the activity of many others, the complex behavioral and physiological processes involved in strategies of animal adaptation are unlikely to be controlled by polymorphisms as simple as the ones proposed by these models. Schmidt-Nielsen, K. (1964), for example, discusses the variety of mechanisms used by *D. merriami* to survive without access to free water or succulent vegetation. The evolution of xeric-adapted kangaroo rats was a lengthy and complex process begun when the ancestral heteromyid stock invaded the evolving desert vegetation of North America. I do not believe that the variation in behavior and physiology described in the preceding sections for *D. microps* may be used as an illustration of any model of adaptation based on simple polymorphisms. Undoubtedly, allele frequencies do accompany the incipient ecological race formation seen in this species. However, my point is that the system as it occurs in nature is quite complex. This complexity requires that the most parsimonious explanation of this variation will be found at the organismic rather than at the molecular level.

Examples of intraspecific variation in resource use are widespread enough among small mammals (Fisler, 1965; Vaughan, 1967; present study) to suggest that many species whose distributions include different biotic communities may display different patterns of adaptation between those communities. This fact is commonly recognized by field mammalogists, although few attempts have been made to incorporate these geographic differences into descriptions of community interactions. Localized studies of small mammal communities (Rosenzweig and Winakur, 1969; Rosenzweig *et al.*, 1975) should be extrapolated to theoretical generalizations with caution. The value and appeal of such practices lie in their applicability to the construction of predictive models. Without such unifying theories, community ecology could not cope with the diversity observed in natural communities. The danger, however, is not only in the pitfall of oversimplification, but in the fact that constant reiteration of these theories will blind ecologists to the adaptive variation present in the species they are seeking to model. In fact, the role of many species in apparently similar communities may display considerable geographic variation. This variation may invalidate predictions of resource allocation or habitat specificity extrapolated from data taken from distant but superficially similar communities. While *D. microps* was selected as a study animal due to an inferred major change in its adaptive strategy between habitats, many other small mammal species display less obvious, although equally significant, differences in niche dimensions between populations. Not only are studies of intraspecific variation in adaptive mechanisms of interest in themselves, but, in this regard, they may be of major importance to the theory of community ecology. It is likely that ecological polymorphism is the rule rather than the exception. A more realistic view of the function of species in diverse communities requires an appreciation of this factor during construction of any predictive model.

SUMMARY AND CONCLUSIONS

The genetic divergence between populations of *Dipodomys microps* was assessed through comparative studies of cranial morphology, tooth morphology, bacular morphology, kidney anatomy, chromosome morphology, and similarity of plasma and liver proteins. The biochemical evidence indicated the genetic distance between populations was related to the geographic distance between them. This is interpreted to suggest recent expansion of the species into its current range from a common ancestral range where there were high levels of gene flow.

Dipodomys microps is an ecologically polymorphic species. The central and western populations shave and eat leaves of *Atriplex confertifolia* as a primary food source. Many southern and eastern populations occur in the *Coleogyne* zone of desert mountain ranges and display a seasonal variation in diet, from a mixed leaf-seed diet in the spring to a primarily or wholly seed diet in late summer and fall.

Laboratory experiments were conducted with adult and captive-born young *D. microps* to investigate the contribution of non-genetic mechanisms of adaptation to differing patterns of resource use between populations of the species from different habitats. Adult *Atriplex* habitat animals predictably used saltbush leaves efficiently as a food item, but never demonstrated any ability to adapt to water-deprived diets. Adult blackbush habitat specimens maintained weight significantly better on dry diets, many individuals gaining weight under such conditions. Few blackbush adults shaved saltbush leaves when first presented with this food item, but if allowed sufficient time to experiment with *Atriplex,* all specimens displayed the species-specific leaf-handling behavior pattern typical of *Atriplex* populations. Leaf-shaving behavior can be expressed in *Coleogyne* zone animals of any age. No irreversible modifications of the phenotype occur during development under field conditions which prevent expression of this inherent behavior pattern. Captive-born young from both habitats were raised with and without exposure to saltbush leaves. No innate superiority in ability to shave these leaves was detected in young from *Atriplex* populations, and young from blackbush populations successfully shaved leaves when given post-weaning experience with this food item.

Both genetic differentiation and a wide range of physiological and behavioral response account for the observed differences in adaptive strategy between phytophagous Owens Valley and granivorous Wolf Hole populations of *D. microps.*

Difficulties experienced in demonstrating the ability of specimens from blackbush habitats to maintain weight on dry seed diets probably resulted from seasonal changes in physiological abilities along with stressful animal room conditions. Only fall-caught Wolf Hole adults tested at Berkeley were able to maintain weight on dry seed diets. These results suggest that water conservation abilities are marginal in these populations, paralleling the situation described for *D. agilis* and *D. venustus.* Under natural circumstances, acclimation to seasonal water stress in blackbush habitats accompanies the drying of the vegetation and the shift to a dry seed diet. In parts of the southern Great Basin the species is restricted to higher elevations where soil moisture and burrow humidity will be high enough to permit survival of the dry season. The species' niche in this zone resembles that of its *heermanni* group relatives.

The genetic homogeneity of the species suggested by enzyme similarity and common tooth morphology explains the ability of blackbush habitat specimens to exhibit the species-specific behavior patterns associated with leaf-shaving when given sufficient opportunity to experiment with this novel food item. However, ecotypic differentiation has progressed far enough to prevent Owens Valley specimens from easily adapting to dry seed regimes, and to prevent Wolf Hole animals from equalling the efficiency with which *Atriplex* habitat specimens use saltbush leaves as a food source.

The adaptation of *D. microps* for *Atriplex* grazing probably occurred in the early Pleistocene following its divergence from *heermanni* group relatives. At this time it invaded the developing Great Basin Desert and was preadapted to leaf-eating by virtue of a moisture dependence common to all *heermanni* group species. This new adaptive strategy was incorporated into the species repertoire without immediately replacing the ancestral seed-eating strategy. During the Wisconsin glaciation, *D. microps* habitat was reduced in the Great Basin and northern Mohavia and the species was compressed into relicts of desert vegetation. A recent warming and drying trend, accompanied by the spread of current vegetation into the Great Basin, allowed reinvasion by a recently-panmictic *Dipodomys microps*. Both the primitive *heermanni* seed-eating strategy and the leaf-eating strategy were common to advancing *D. microps* populations. Selection since reinvasion of the Mojave and Great Basin Deserts has produced incipient stages of ecological race formation.

The population of *D. microps* in Joshua Tree National Monument has a unique karyotype. The close relationship detected with neighboring populations by biochemical methods suggests this karyotypic change is a recent event. The presence of characteristic tooth morphology and assignment of these specimens to *D. m. occidentalis* on the basis of cranial measurements indicates an origin in an *Atriplex*-adapted population. Palaeoecological evidence that these southern highlands were unsuitable habitat for *D. microps* until recently suggests that this karyotypic form is derived from the biarmed karyotype following invasion of this habitat after the Wisconsin glaciation. Were the karyotype of the Joshua Tree form ancestral, other populations bearing this relictual karyotype should have been detected in similar southern refugia. Similarity of the Joshua Tree karyotype with that of the broad-faced *heermanni* subgroup species is therefore held to be convergent.

The presence of intraspecific differences in adaptive mechanisms implies that theories of community ecology that do not take these differences into account will erroneously predict the roles of species in community structure in habitats other than those included in the data base for that particular theory.

Earlier studies have demonstrated the presence of intraspecific differences in physiology in small mammals. Similarly, earlier works have amply documented intraspecific variation, as measured by a variety of systematic criteria. The significance of the present analysis is that it documents an ecological polymorphism in a vertebrate species and indicates both the genetic and non-genetic components contributing to the achievement of that polymorphism. I suggest that most wide-ranging species display ecological polymorphisms to a greater or lesser degree, and that adaptations allowing these differences in realized niche are accomplished, as in *D. microps,* by a combination of ecotypic and ecophenic adaptation. I believe that the careful study of genetic and phenotypic components of ecological variation in animal species will be as productive to zoology as the genecological studies initiated by Göte Turesson have been to botany.

Appendix: Specimens Examined

CRANIAL VARIATION

Dipodomys microps microps, 12: CALIFORNIA. Inyo Co.: Silver Canyon, 3; Bishop Creek, 1; 1 mi. NW Lone Pine, 2; Lone Pine Station, 2½ mi. NE Lone Pine, 1; Mazourka Canyon, 7700 ft., Inyo Mts., 1; 1½ mi. SE Olancha, 4. *Dipodomys microps occidentalis,* 20: CALIFORNIA. San Bernardino Co.: SE side Clark Mtn., 5100 ft., 2. NEVADA. Lincoln Co.: 21 mi. W Panaca, Desert Valley, 5300 ft., 2; Crystal Springs, 4000 ft., Pahranagat Valley, 5; 2 mi. E Crystal Springs, 2; 5 mi. E Crystal Springs, 1; 8 mi. SW Hancock Summit, 5300 ft., 2; 5½ mi. N Summit Springs, 4700 ft., 1; 16 mi. E Groom Baldy, 1; 14½ mi. S Groom Baldy, 2. Nye Co.: N shore Mud Lake, 5300 ft., SE end Ralston Valley, 1; Stonewall Flat, 4700 ft., 14 mi. SE Goldfield, 1. *Dipodomys microps celsus,* 12: ARIZONA. Mohave Co.: near S boundary Kaibab Indian Res., 3; Kanab Wash, S boundary Kaibab Indian Res., 1; 10 mi. N Wolf Hole, 8. *Dipodomys microps ssp.,* 11: CALIFORNIA. Riverside Co.: 1¼ mi. NE Stubby Springs, 11 (three from Natural History Museum of Los Angeles County).

TOOTH MORPHOLOGY

Dipodomys microps centralis, 21 (*Atriplex* zone sample): NEVADA. Lincoln Co.: 17 mi. N Groom Baldy, Penoyer Valley, 5; 14 mi. NNW Groom Baldy, 1; 9 mi. W Groom Baldy, 5500 ft., 15. *Dipodomys microps celsus,* 21 (*Coleogyne* zone sample): ARIZONA. Mohave Co.: near S boundary Kaibab Indian Res., 3; Kanab Wash, S boundary Kaibab Indian Res., 1; 10 mi. N Wolf Hole, 17.

BACULAR VARIATION

Dipodomys microps microps, 7: CALIFORNIA. Inyo Co.: 1 mi. E Laws, 2; 2 mi. E Big Pine, 1. Kern Co.: 12¾ mi. W Randsberg, 4. *Dipodomys microps occidentalis,* 2: CALIFORNIA. San Bernardino Co.: SE side Clark Mountain, 5100 ft., 2. *Dipodomys microps celsus,* 5: ARIZONA. Mohave Co.: 10 mi. N Wolf Hole, 5. *Dipodomys microps ssp.,* 4: CALIFORNIA. Riverside Co.: 1¼ mi. NE Stubby Springs, 3. San Bernardino Co.: 3 mi. NW Yucca Valley, 1.

KIDNEY ANATOMY

Dipodomys microps microps, 10: CALIFORNIA. Inyo Co.: 1 mi. E Laws, 9; 2 mi. E Big Pine, 1. *Dipodomys microps celsus,* 13: ARIZONA. Mohave Co.: 10 mi. N Wolf Hole, 13.

CHROMOSOMAL VARIATION

Dipodomys microps microps, 10: CALIFORNIA. Inyo Co.: 2 mi. E Big Pine, 2. Kern Co.: 12¾ mi. W Randsberg, 7. Los Angeles Co.: 6 mi. N Lancaster, 1. *Dipodomys microps occidentalis,* 2: CALIFORNIA. San Bernardino Co.: ½ mi. W Horse Thief Springs, Kingston Range, 1. NEVADA. Lander Co.: 2 mi. W Railroad Pass, Smith Creek Valley, 1. *Dipodomys microps centralis,* 1: NEVADA. White Pine Co.: 5½ mi. NW Shoshone, 1. *Dipodomys microps celsus,* 3: ARIZONA. Mohave Co.: 10 mi. N Wolf Hole, 3. *Dipodomys microps woodburyi,* 2: UTAH. Washington Co.: W slope Beaverdam Mountains, 3800 ft., 2. *Dipodomys microps ssp.,* 7: CALIFORNIA. Riverside Co.: 1¼ mi. NE Stubby Springs, 6. San Bernardino Co.: 3 mi. NE Yucca Valley, 1.

BIOCHEMICAL VARIATION

Dipodomys microps microps, 3: CALIFORNIA. Inyo Co.: 2 mi. E Big Pine, 2. Los Angeles Co.: 6 mi. N Lancaster, 1. *Dipodomys microps celsus,* 4: ARIZONA. Mohave Co.: 10 mi. N Wolf Hole, 4. *Dipodomys microps occidentalis,* 2: CALIFORNIA. San Bernardino Co.: ½ mi. W Horse Thief Springs, Kingston Range, 1. NEVADA. Lander Co.: 2 mi. W Railroad Pass, Smith Creek Valley, 1. *Dipodomys microps centralis,* 1: NEVADA. White Pine Co.: 5¼ mi. NW Shoshone, 1. *Dipodomys microps woodburyi,* 2: UTAH. Washington Co.: W slope Beaverdam Mountains, 3800 ft., 2. *Dipodomys microps ssp.,* 4: CALIFORNIA. Riverside Co.: 1¼ mi. NE Stubby Springs, 3. San Bernardino Co.: 3 mi. NW Yucca Valley, 1.

Literature Cited

AL-ANI, H. A., B. R. STRAIN, and H. A. MOONEY
    1972. The physiological ecology of diverse populations of the desert shrub *Simmondsia chinensis*. J. Ecol., 60:41-57.

ALCOZE, T. M., and E. G. ZIMMERMAN
    1973. Food habits and dietary overlap of two heteromyid rodents from the mesquite plains of Texas. J. Mamm., 54:900-908.

ANDERSON, A. O., and D. M. ALLRED
    1964. Kangaroo rat burrows at the Nevada Test Site. Great Basin Natur., 24:93-101.

AXELROD, D. I.
    1950. Evolution of desert vegetation in western North America. Carnegie Instn. Publ. No. 590:217-306.

BAKER, H. G.
    1965. Characteristics and modes of origin of weeds. Pp. 147-172, *in* H. G. Baker and G. L. Stebbins, eds., The genetics of colonizing species. Academic Press, New York.
    1974. The evolution of weeds. Pp. 1-24, *in* R. F. Johnston, ed., Annual Review of Ecology and Systematics. Annual Reviews, Palo Alto.

BAUER, H. L.
    1936. Moisture relations in the chaparral of the Santa Monica Mountains, California. Ecol. Monogr., 6:409-454.
    1943. The statistical analysis of chaparral and other plant communities by means of transect samples. Ecology, 24:45-60.

BAUMGARTNER, L. L., and A. C. MARTIN
    1939. Plant histology as an aid in squirrel food-habit studies. J. Wildl. Mgmt., 3:266-268.

BEATLEY, J. C.
    1969. Dependence of desert rodents on winter annuals and precipitation. Ecology, 50:721-724.
    1976a. Rainfall and fluctuating plant populations in relation to distributions and numbers of desert rodents in southern Nevada. Oecologia, 24:21-42.
    1976b. Environments of kangaroo rats (*Dipodomys*) and effects of environmental change on populations in southern Nevada. J. Mamm., 57:67-93.

BEST, T. L., and G. D. SCHNELL
    1974. Bacular variation in kangaroo rats (genus Dipodomys). Amer. Midland Natur., 91:257-270.

BILLINGS, W. D.
    1949. The shadscale vegetation zone of Nevada and eastern California in relation to climate and soils. Amer. Midland Natur., 42:87-109.

BRADLEY, W. G., and R. A. MAUER
    1971. Reproduction and food habits of Merriam's Kangaroo Rat, *Dipodomys merriami*. J. Mamm., 52:497-507.

BROWN, J. H.
    1973. Species diversity of seed-eating desert rodents in sand dune habitats. Ecology, 54:775-787.

1975. Geographical ecology of desert rodents. Pp. 315-341, in M. L. Cody and J. M. Diamond, eds., Ecology and evolution of communities. Harvard Univ. Press, Cambridge.

BROWNFIELD, M. S., and B. A. WUNDER
1976. Relative medullary area: a new structural index for estimating urinary concentrating capacity of mammals. Comp. Biochem. Physiol., 55A:69-75.

CADE, T. J., and G. A. BARTHOLOMEW
1959. Sea-water and salt utilization by Savannah Sparrows. Physiol. Zool., 32:230-238.

CARPENTER, R. E.
1966. A comparison of thermoregulation and water metabolism in the kangaroo rats Dipodomys agilis and Dipodomys merriami. Univ. California Publ. Zool., 78:1-36.
1969. Structure and function of the kidney and the water balance of desert bats. Physiol. Zool., 42:288-302.

CHEW, R. M.
1958. Reproduction by *Dipodomys merriami* in captivity. J. Mamm., 39:597-598.

CHURCH, R. L.
1969. Evaporative water loss and gross effects of water privation in the kangaroo rat, *Dipodomys venustus*. J. Mamm., 50:514-523.

CLAUSEN, J., and W. M. HIESEY
1958. Experimental studies on the nature of species. IV. Genetic structure of ecological races. Publ. Carnegie Instn., No. 615.

CLAUSEN, J., D. D. KECK, and W. M. HIESEY
1940. Experimental studies on the nature of species. I. Effect of varied environments on western North American plants. Publ. Carnegie Instn., No. 520.
1948. Experimental studies on the nature of species. III. Environmental responses of climatic races of *Achillea*. Publ. Carnegie Instn., No. 581.

CSUTI, B. A.
1971. Karyotypes of kangaroo rats from southern California. J. Mamm., 52:202-206.
1977. Patterns of adaptation and variation in the Great Basin Kangaroo Rat (*Dipodomys microps*). Unpublished Ph.D. dissertation. Univ. of California, Berkeley.

ECOLOGY AND EPIZOOLOGY RESEARCH GROUP, UNIVERSITY OF UTAH
1968. A study of the ecology and epizoology of the native fauna of the Great Salt Lake Desert: Annual summary review, 1968.

EISENBERG, J. F.
1963. The behavior of heteromyid rodents. Univ. California Publ. Zool., 69:1-100.

FAUTIN, R. W.
1946. Biotic communities of the northern desert shrub biome in western Utah. Ecol. Monogr., 16:251-310.

FISLER, G. F.
1965. Adaptations and speciation in harvest mice of the marshes of San Francisco Bay. Univ. California Publ. Zool., 77:1-108.

FLAKE, L. D.
1973. Food habits of four species of rodents on a short-grass prairie in Colorado. J. Mamm., 54:636-647.

FLEMING, T. H.
1977. Response of two species of tropical heteromyid rodents to reduced food and water availability. J. Mamm., 58:102-106.

GENOWAYS, H. H., and J. K. JONES, JR.
1971. Systematics of southern banner-tailed kangaroo rats of the *Dipodomys phillipsii* group. J. Mamm., 52:265-287.

GOLDMAN, E. A.
1924. Two new kangaroo rats from Arizona. Jour. Washington Acad. Sci., 14:372-373.

GREEGOR, D. H., JR.
1975. Renal capabilities of an Argentine desert armadillo. J. Mamm., 56:626-632.

GREGOR, J. W.
1944. The ecotype. Biol. Rev., 19:20-30.
1946. Ecotypic differentiation. New Phytologist, 45:254-270.

GRINNELL, J.
- 1922. A geographical study of the kangaroo rats of California. Univ. California Publ. Zool., 24:1-124.
- 1933. Review of the recent mammal fauna of California. Univ. California Publ. Zool., 40:71-234.

HALL, E. R.
- 1946. Mammals of Nevada. Univ. of California Press, Berkeley.

HALL, E. R., and F. H. DALE
- 1939. Geographic races of the kangaroo rat, Dipodomys microps. Occas. Papers Mus. Zool., Louisiana State Univ., 4:47-63.

HALL, E. R., and K. R. KELSON
- 1959. The mammals of North America. Ronald Press, New York.

HANSSON, L.
- 1970. Methods of morphological diet micro-analysis in rodents. Oikos, 21:255-266.

HARDY, R.
- 1945. The influence of types of soil upon the local distribution of some mammals in southwestern Utah. Ecol. Monogr., 15:71-108.
- 1949. Notes on mammals from Arizona, Nevada, and Utah. J. Mamm., 30:434-435.

HARRISON, D. L.
- 1972. The mammals of Arabia, Vol. 3. Ernest Benn Ltd., London.

HARRISON, G. A.
- 1959. Environmental determination of the phenotype. Pp. 81-86, in A. J. Cain, ed., Function and taxonomic importance. Systematics Assoc. Publ., No. 3.

HATCH, F. T., E. J. RIDLEY, and J. A. MAZRIMAS
- 1971. Some *Dipodomys* species: Ecologic and taxonomic features, estrous cycle, and breeding attempts. Bio-Medical Division, Lawrence Livermore Laboratory, Livermore.

HESLOP-HARRISON, J.
- 1964. Forty years of genecology. Pp. 159-247, in J. B. Cragg, ed., Adv. in Ecol. Res., Vol. 2.

HUTCHINSON, G. E.
- 1957. Concluding remarks. Cold Spring Harbor Symposium on Quantitative Biology, No. 22:415-427.

JOHNSON, D. H., M. D. BRYANT, and A. H. MILLER
- 1948. Vertebrate animals of the Providence Mountains area of California. Univ. California Publ. Zool., 48:221-376.

JOHNSON, D. R.
- 1961. The food habits of rodents on rangelands of southern Idaho. Ecology, 42:407-410.

JOHNSON, O. W., and R. D. OHMART
- 1973. Some features of water economy and kidney microstructure in the Large-billed Savannah Sparrow (Passerculus sandwichensis rostratus). Physiol. Zool., 46:276-284.

JOHNSON, W. E., and R. K. SELANDER
- 1971. Protein variation and systematics in kangaroo rats (genus *Dipodomys*). Syst. Zool., 20:377-405.

KELLY, T. S.
- 1969. The comparative morphology of the male phallus in the genus *Dipodomys*. Unpublished M. S. thesis, California State University, Northridge.

KENAGY, G. J.
- 1972. Saltbush leaves: excision of hypersaline tissue by a kangaroo rat. Science, 178:1094-1096.
- 1973a. Daily and seasonal patterns of activity and energetics in a heteromyid rodent community. Ecology, 54:1201-1219.
- 1973b. Adaptations for leaf eating in the Great Basin Kangaroo Rat, *Dipodomys microps*. Oecologia, 12:383-412.

KING, T. J., JR.
- 1976. Late Pleistocene-early Holocene history of coniferous woodlands in the Lucerne Valley region, Mohave Desert, California. Great Basin Natur., 36:227-238.

LACKEY, J. A.
    1967a. Growth and development of *Dipodomys stephensi.* J. Mamm., 48:624-632.
    1967b. Biosystematics of *heermanni* group kangaroo rats in southern California. Trans. San Diego Soc. Nat. Hist., 14:313-344.

LANDRY, S. O., JR.
    1970. The Rodentia as omnivores. Quart. Rev. Biol., 45:351-372.

LARRISON, E. J., and D. R. JOHNSON
    1973. Density changes and habitat affinities of rodents of shadscale and sagebrush associations. Great Basin Natur., 33:255-264.

LEVINS, R.
    1963. Theory of fitness in a heterogeneous environment II. Developmental flexibility and niche selection. Amer. Natur., 97:75-90.
    1968. Evolution in changing environments. Princeton Univ. Press, Princeton.

LIDICKER, W. Z., JR.
    1960a. An analysis of intraspecific variation in the kangaroo rat Dipodomys merriami. Univ. California Publ. Zool., 67:125-218.
    1960b. The baculum of *Dipodomys ornatus* and its implication for superspecific groupings of kangaroo rats. J. Mamm., 41:495-499.

LINCOLN, F. C.
    1930. Calculating waterfowl abundance on the basis of banding returns. Circ. U. S. Dept. of Agric., 118:1-4.

LINDEBORG, R. G.
    1952. Water requirements of certain rodents from xeric and mesic habitats. Contr. Lab. Vert. Biol., Univ. Michigan No. 58:1-32.

LUDWIG, W.
    1950. Zur theorie der konkurrenz. Die annidation (Einnischung) als fünfter Evolutionsfaktor. Pp. 516-537, *in* W. Herre, ed., Neue Ergeb. Probleme Zool., Klatt-Festschrift 1950. Akad. Verlagsgesellschaft, Geest and Portig K.-G., Leipzig.

LYNCH, G. R., C. B. LYNCH, M. DUBE, and C. ALLEN
    1976. Early cold exposure: effects on behavioral and physiological thermoregulation in the house mouse, Mus musculus. Physiol. Zool., 49:191-199.

MAC ARTHUR, R. H.
    1958. Population ecology of some warblers of northeastern coniferous forests. Ecology, 39:599-619.

MAC MILLEN, R. E.
    1964. Population ecology, water relations, and social behavior of a southern California semidesert rodent fauna. Univ. California Publ. Zool., 71:1-59.

MAC MILLEN, R. E., and E. A. CHRISTOPHER
    1975. The water relations of two populations of noncaptive desert rodents. Pp. 117-137, *in* N. F. Hadley, ed., Environmental physiology of desert organisms. Dowden, Hutchinson, and Ross, Stroudsberg.

MARES, M. A.
    1975. Observations of Argentine desert rodent ecology, with emphasis on water relations of *Eligmodontia typus.* Pp. 155-175, *in* I. Prakash and P. K. Ghosh, eds., Rodents in desert environments. W. Junk, The Hague.

MARTIN, P. S., and P. J. MEHRINGER, JR.
    1965. Pleistocene pollen analysis and biogeography of the southwest. Pp. 433-451, *in* H. E. Wright and D. G. Frey, eds., The Quaternary of the United States. Princeton Univ. Press, Princeton.

MARVIN, C. F.
    1941. Psychrometric tables for obtaining the vapor pressure, relative humidity, and temperature of the dew-point. U. S. Govt. Printing Office, Washington.

MASON, E. B.
    1974. Metabolic responses of two species of Peromyscus raised in different thermal environments. Physiol. Zool., 47:68-74.

MATTHEY, R.
    1951. The chromosomes of the vertebrates. Pp. 159-180, *in* M. Demerec, ed., Advances in genetics, Vol. 4. Academic Press, New York.

MAYR, E.
    1963. Animal species and evolution. Harvard Univ. Press, Cambridge.
MAZA, B. G., N. R. FRENCH, and A. P. ASCHWANDEN
    1973. Home range dynamics in a population of heteromyid rodents. J. Mamm., 54: 405-425.
MEHRINGER, P. J., JR.
    1967. Pollen analysis of the Tule Springs area, Nevada. Pp. 129-200, in H. M. Wormington and D. Ellis, eds., Pleistocene studies in southern Nevada. Nevada State Museum Anthropological Papers, No. 13, Carson City.
    1977. Great Basin late Quaternary environments and chronology. Pp. 113-167, in D. D. Fowler, ed., Models and Great Basin prehistory. Desert Research Institute Publications in the Social Sciences, No. 12. University of Nevada, Reno.
MERRIAM, C. H.
    1904. New and little known kangaroo rats of the genus *Perodipus*. Proc. Biol. Soc. Washington, 17:139-145.
MILLER, A. H., and R. C. STEBBINS
    1964. The lives of desert animals in Joshua Tree National Monument. Univ. California Press, Berkeley.
MOONEY, H. A., and F. SHROPSHIRE
    1967. Population variability in temperature related photosynthetic acclimation. Oecologia Plantarum, 2:1-13.
MULLEN, R. K.
    1971. Energy metabolism and body water turnover rates of two species of free-living kangaroo rats, *Dipodomys merriami* and *Dipodomys microps*. Comp. Biochem. Physiol., 39A:379-390.
MUNZ, P. A., and D. D. KECK
    1959. A California flora. Univ. California Press, Berkeley.
MURIE, M.
    1961. Metabolic characteristics of mountain, desert and coastal populations of Peromyscus. Ecology, 42:723-740.
NEI, M.
    1971. Interspecific gene differences and evolutionary time evaluated from electrophoretic data on protein identity. Amer. Natur., 105:385-398.
NELSON, J. F., and R. M. CHEW
    1977. Factors affecting seed reserves in the soil of a Mojave Desert ecosystem, Rock Valley, Nye County, Nevada. Amer. Midland Natur., 97:300-320.
NICHTER, R.
    1957. The effect of variation in humidity and water intake on activity of *Dipodomys*. J. Mamm., 38:502-512.
PATTON, J. L.
    1967. Chromosome studies of certain pocket mice, genus *Perognathus* (Rodentia: Heteromyidae). J. Mamm., 48:27-37.
    1969. Chromosome evolution in the pocket mouse, *Perognathus goldmani* Osgood. Evolution, 23:645-662.
REICHMAN, O. J.
    1975. Relation of desert rodent diets to available resources. J. Mamm., 56:731-751.
    1977. Optimization of diets through food preferences by heteromyid rodents. Ecology, 58:454-457.
REAKA, M. L., and K. B. ARMITAGE
    1976. The water economy of harvest mice from xeric and mesic environments. Physiol. Zool., 49:307-327.
ROSENZWEIG, M. L., B. SMIGEL, and A. KRAFT
    1975. Patterns of food, space and diversity. Pp. 241-268, in I. Prakash and P. K. Ghosh, eds., Rodents in desert environments. W. Junk, The Hague.
ROSENZWEIG, M. L., and J. WINAKUR
    1969. Population ecology of desert rodent communities: habitats and environmental complexity. Ecology, 50:558-572.

ROSS, L. G.
    1930. A comparative study of daily water-intake among certain taxonomic and geographic groups within the genus Peromyscus. Biol. Bull., 59:326-338.

SAMPSON, A. W., and B. S. JESPERSEN
    1963. California range brushlands and browse plants. California Agricultural Experiment Station Extension Service Manual 33.

SARICH, V. M.
    1977. Rates, sample sizes, and the neutrality hypothesis for electrophoresis in evolutionary studies. Nature, 265:24-28.

SCHMIDT-NIELSEN, B.
    1964. Organ systems in adaptation: the excretory system. Pp. 215-243, in D. B. Dill, ed., Handbook of physiology, Sec. 4: Adaptation to the environment. Amer. Physiol. Soc., Washington.

SCHMIDT-NIELSEN, B., and R. O'DELL
    1961. Structure and concentrating mechanism in the mammalian kidney. Amer. J. Physiology, 200:1119-1124.

SCHMIDT-NIELSEN, B., and K. SCHMIDT-NIELSEN
    1950. Evaporative water loss in desert rodents in their natural habitat. Ecology, 31:75-85.

SCHMIDT-NIELSEN, K.
    1964. Desert Animals. Physiological problems of heat and water. Oxford Univ. Press, Fair Lawn.

SCHMIDT-NIELSEN, K., and B. SCHMIDT-NIELSEN
    1952. Water metabolism of desert mammals. Physiol. Rev., 32:135-166.

SELANDER, R. K., M. H. SMITH, S. Y. YANG, W. E. JOHNSON, and J. B. GENTRY
    1971. IV. Biochemical polymorphism and systematics in the genus *Peromyscus*. I. Variation in the Old-field Mouse (*Peromyscus polionotus*). Studies in Genetics VI, Univ. Texas Publ. 7103.

SETZER, H. W.
    1949. Subspeciation in the kangaroo rat, Dipodomys ordii. Univ. Kansas Publ., Mus. Nat. Hist., 1:473-573.

SHANNON, C. E., and W. WEAVER
    1949. The mathematical theory of communication. Univ. of Illinois Press, Urbana.

SMITH, M. H.
    1968. A comparison of different methods of capturing and estimating numbers of mice. J. Mamm., 49:455-462.

SOHOLT, L. F.
    1977. Consumption of herbaceous vegetation and water during reproduction and development of Merriam's kangaroo rat, Dipodomys merriami. Amer. Midland Natur., 98:445-457.

SOKAL, R. R., and F. J. ROHLF
    1969. Biometrics. W. H. Freeman, San Francisco.

SPARKS, D. R., and J. C. MALECHECK
    1968. Estimating percentage dry weight in diets using a microscopic technique. J. Range Mgmt., 21:264-265.

STOCK, A. D.
    1970. Notes on mammals of southwestern Utah. J. Mamm., 51:429-433.
    1974. Chromosome evolution in the genus *Dipodomys* and its taxonomic and phylogenetic implications. J. Mamm., 55:505-526.

SUMNER, F. B.
    1924. The stability of subspecific characters under changed conditions of environment. Amer. Natur., 58:481-505.
    1932. Genetic, distributional, and evolutionary studies of the subspecies of deer mice (Peromyscus). Biblio. Genetica, 9:1-106.

TAPPE, D. T.
    1941. Natural history of the Tulare kangaroo rat. J. Mamm., 22:117-148.

TURESSON, G.
    1919. The cause of plagiotropy in maritime shore plants. Lunds Universitets Årsskrift, NF. Avd. 2., Bd. 16, Nr. 2.

1923. The scope and import of genecology. Hereditas, 4:171-176.
UNITED STATES DEPARTMENT OF AGRICULTURE
1963. Composition of foods, Agricultural Handbook No. 8. Consumer food and economics research division, U.S.D.A.
UNITED STATES WEATHER BUREAU
1964. Climatography of the United States. Supplement for 1951-60. No. 86-4.
1965. Climatography of the United States. Supplement for 1951-60. No. 86-37.
VAUGHAN, T. A.
1967. Food habits of the northern pocket gopher on shortgrass prairie. Amer. Midland Natur., 77:176-189.
VORHIES, C. T., and W. P. TAYLOR
1922. Life history of the kangaroo rat *Dipodomys spectabilis spectabilis* Merriam. U.S.D.A. Bull. No. 1091.
WARNOCK, R. G., and A. W. GRUNDMAN
1963. Food habits of some small mammals of the Bonneville Basin as determined by the contents of the stomach and intestine. Proc. Utah Acad. Sci., Arts, and Letters, 40:66-73.
WELLS, P. V., and R. BERGER
1967. Late Pleistocene history of coniferous woodland in the Mohave Desert. Science, 155:1640-1647.
WILSON, A. D.
1966a. The value of *Atriplex* (saltbush) and *Kochia* (bluebush) species as food for sheep. Aust. J. Agric. Res., 17:147-153.
1966b. The intake and excretion of sodium by sheep fed on species of *Atriplex* (saltbush) and *Kochia* (bluebush). Aust. J. Agric. Res., 17:155-163.

Plates

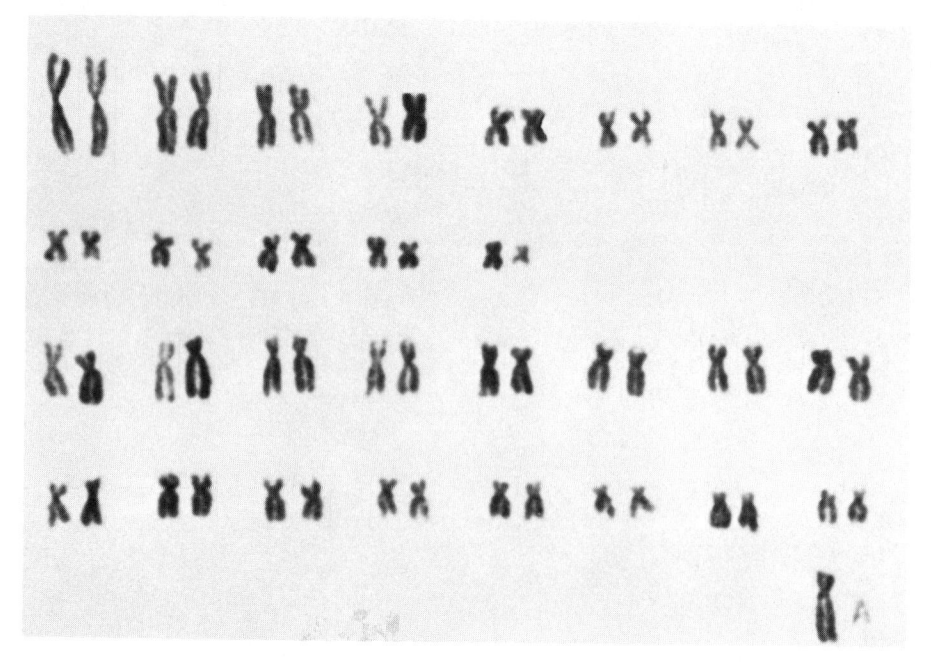

Plate 1a. Karyotype of *Dipodomys microps microps*, male, from 12¾ mi. W Randsberg, Kern Co., California.

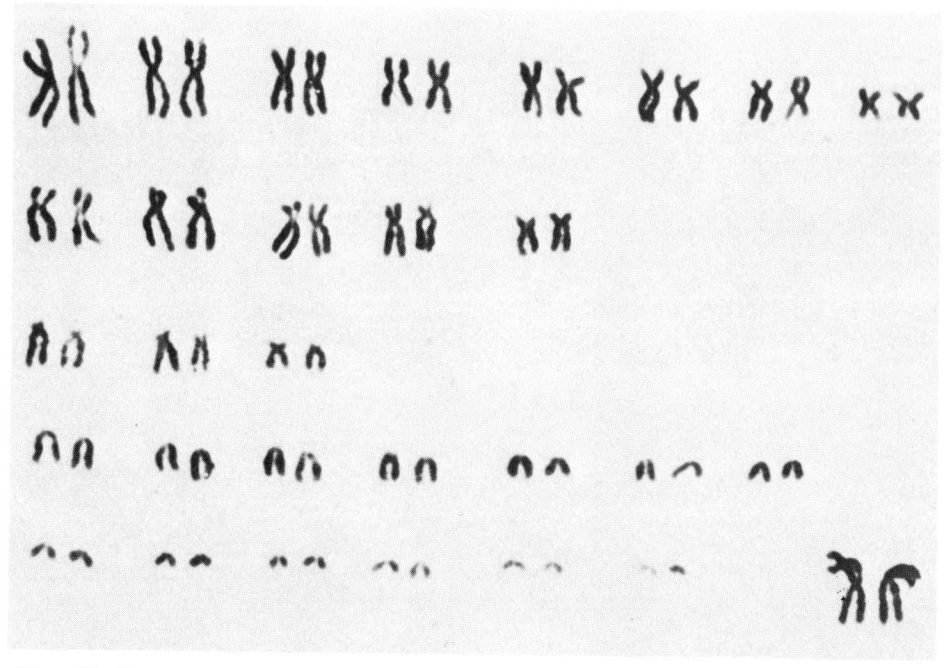

Plate 1b. Karyotype of *Dipodomys microps*, female, from 1¼ mi. NE Stubby Springs, Riverside Co., California. All specimens taken from Juniper Flats, Joshua Tree National Monument, have this karyotype.

Plate 2a. Study site two miles east of Big Pine, Inyo Co., California. This view, looking west toward the Sierra Nevada, shows *Atriplex confertifolia* bushes in the foreground. Note the absence of herbaceous vegetation. A few taller *Sarcobatus* bushes can be seen in the background.

Plate 2b. Study area 10 miles north of Wolf Hole, Mohave Co., Arizona. This site is in the foothills of the eastern slope of the Virgin Mountains. *Yucca, Lycium,* and *Coleogyne* are the most frequent shrubs.